SAINTS *alive!*

Healing in the Church

SAINTS *alive!*

Healing in the Church

LEADERS MANUAL

ROGER M. VAUGHAN

provider
helping you to help others

ISBN 1 84291 040 X

Published by
KINGSWAY COMMUNICATIONS LTD
Lottbridge Drove, Eastbourne, BN23 6NT, England.
Email: books@kingsway.co.uk
in association with
Anglican Renewal Ministries
4 Bramble Street, Derby DE1 1HU.
Email: saintsalive@anglican-renewal.org.uk

Book design and production for the publishers by
Bookprint Creative Services, P.O. Box 827, BN21 3YJ, England.
Printed in Great Britain.

Contents

Preface

For over a decade *Saints for Healing* helped many local churches establish a healing ministry. The course gave people a basic understanding of Christian healing. During the period that *Saints for Healing* was in print, the church's acceptance of this ministry grew and, inevitably, moved on. The launch of a revised series of courses under the generic title of *Saints Alive!* has provided a much-needed opportunity to update this teaching course on the Christian healing ministry.

The last ten years has seen a general acceptance that there is more to healing than simply the application of medical principles. Alternative and complementary methods of healing abound, and some have gained credibility with medical practitioners as well as the general public. In what ways is the Christian ministry of healing different from other alternative healing practices?

In our 'postmodern' society, people are searching for meaning to life through diverse spiritual practices – some of them malign. Many of these seekers find their way into Christian churches. How can we welcome them, and at the same time challenge them about the effects of their past spiritual experimentation? How can we make use of their undoubted gifts, often expressed in terms of healing, yet help them to see that Christian healing is (as Morris Maddocks writes) 'Jesus Christ meeting us at our point of need'? New material in *Saints Alive! Healing in the Church* looks at these questions.

In the 1980s many books were published that laid down the foundations of our understanding of the Christian healing ministry. These have not been superseded but there has been a growing emphasis on good practice in this ministry.

Guidelines for good practice, and liturgies that reflect it, have been produced. *Common Worship – Pastoral Services* (Church House Publishing 2000) provides a whole section of services for wholeness and healing. These include a short service entitled 'Prayers for protection and peace'. The recognition that deliverance from evil is part of the journey towards wholeness is restoring such deliverance to its proper place within the Christian ministry of healing. This trend is reflected in the report *A Time to Heal* (Church House Publishing 2000) where, once again, stress is laid on the principles of good practice in this work of the kingdom. *Saints Alive! Healing in the Church* is able to reflect these important shifts in our thinking and practice.

Jesus, through the Holy Spirit, still calls the church to preach the coming of the kingdom and to heal the sick. It is my prayer that God will use this revised course to introduce many people to the Christian ministry of healing, and to enable local churches to develop it in a way which will bring healing and wholeness to individuals, and honour and glory to God.

Roger M. Vaughan

Introduction

▶ The aim of the course

This course aims to provide a general foundation to the Christian ministry of healing. It seeks to encourage all who take part in the course to become personally involved in this ministry. It points to ways in which this ministry may be developed both individually and corporately.

▶ The shape of the course

It may be helpful to think of the course in three phases:

- Some basic foundation material (Sessions 1–4).
- A transition where the group members begin to see how the foundation material applies to them personally, and how they can become more involved in the Christian ministry of healing themselves (Sessions 5–6).
- The practical outworking, both for individuals and for the local church (Sessions 8–9).

Session 7, 'God and the mystery of suffering', stands on its own and its position could be transposed if you feel that your group needs to explore some of the difficult questions about suffering earlier on in the course. Because the link-work is designed to follow on from the group session each week, you would have to ask your group members to use the material for week 7 after you had worked through the session, wherever it came in the course.

▶ The pattern for each session

Each session follows the same format and the contents are sum-marised at the beginning of the chapter. The Leaders Manual follows this pattern in its presentation. In general each session com-prises the following.

- Introductions and prayer.
- The main learning focus for the session.
- Practical teaching on ways of praying for healing.
- Concluding worship.

At the end of each session there is a list of available resources.

▶ Group discussion

These are not the only occasions when there will be group partici-pation, but these sections give the leader ideas for helping the group to work on material which has just been presented.

▶ Timing of the sessions

The times which are given with the summaries are only a guide. You should, however, keep to a definite finishing time. Following the lead of *Saints Alive! Life in the Spirit*, the first course in this series, a session time of 90 minutes is suggested. However, the authors also stress the importance of a certain flexibility about timing. 'Good meetings are like football matches – 90 minutes with 30 minutes' extra time if needed.' Don't try to cover every piece of teaching or group exercise. To help you tailor the course to your particular needs, we have incorporated some optional material.

▶ Optional material

Each session has some parts marked 'optional'. It is suggested that if you wish to cut back on the amount of material you present you leave these sections out first. Some may need to be omitted because they are not suitable to your own group's needs (eg some of the material on deliverance ministry in Session 8). Use the course as a resource and design your own sessions to fit the unique needs of your church or group.

▶ Preparation for each session

Carefully read through the session notes, and through some of the material listed in the resources section. Allow this reading to soak in during the week before the session, and make it part of your prayer preparation. Decide if there are sections which you need to adapt or omit. Leaders should take part fully in the link-work readings.

▶ Introducing the link-work books

Go through the link-work book introduction with your group members. If you are familiar with the *Saints Alive! Life in the Spirit* link-work books take note of the slight changes that have been made in the format of this book. In particular:

- The incorporation of the 'chunk reading' into days 6 and 7 of each week's readings.
- The provision of a verse for contemplation on day 4.
- The various appendices.

▶ Leadership

The following points should be borne in mind:

- Mature leadership is vital.
- It is strongly advisable to have at least two leaders.
- If the leadership is shared then it is vital for the leaders to meet for planning between sessions.
- Leadership will combine teaching, enabling, leading in worship and pastoral care of the group.

Reference to the *Saints Alive! Life in the Spirit* Leaders Manual will be extremely helpful. Many of the suggestions in the introduction to this first course in the series, by John Finney and Felicity Lawson, apply to the subsequent courses in the series and are taken as read! The introduction to John and Felicity's book will give many guidelines to help you present this course more effectively.

▶ The questionnaire

The simple questionnaire in Appendix A of the link-work book is intended to achieve the following:

- Reveal where each group member is in terms of their understanding of the Christian healing ministry.
- Discover if group members have been involved with any other form of non-medical healing.
- Help the group members to think through any questions about which they are still uncertain.
- Give leaders valuable insights into the pastoral care which may be needed by some of the group members.

▶ Presentation

Imaginative and varied presentation is most important.

- Encourage members to take an active part in the prayers and worship as soon as possible.
- Where possible, delegate part of the worship time to group members.
- Pilot groups using this material have found that a coffee or tea break in the middle of the session has been an excellent alternative to refreshments at the end. However, if you do this you will need to arrange for someone not on the course to prepare the refreshments, as discussion tends to go on during the break!
- Be aware that courses on healing can attract people who have had, or are having, some experience of occult healing.
- Set up an overhead projector so that you can make use of the visual aids.
- Use personal testimony wherever you can.

- It is quite possible that you will have one or two people in the group who already have quite a lot of experience in this ministry. Enlist their help in the teaching and leading of worship.

▶ New material

This revision of the previous *Saints for Healing* course contains new material. This includes introductions to the following:

- Alternative therapies. Are they counterfeit? How can we tell? (Session 3.)
- Wider consideration of the problems raised when things get tough (Session 4).
- Prayer in the face of chronic illness and pain (Session 7).
- Guidelines for good practice in this ministry (Session 8).
- An optional section on helping people involved in the occult (Session 8).
- Helping the local church think through the issues raised in moving towards a ministry of prayer for healing (Session 9).

▶ OHP material

We have provided OHP masters in Appendix G which we hope will aid presentation of the material. Usually the content of the OHP material is also set out as part of the text. You have permission to reproduce these masters on transparencies for your own use.

▶ Preliminary meeting

An explanatory session before the formal start of the course lets people have a sight of the link-work books and provides an opportunity for questions.

This meeting may only take 30–45 minutes, perhaps after a service in church, but it is *essential*, both to sort out the practical details and also to set the 'tone' of the course. Prospective members should be encouraged to attend this preliminary meeting.

It has been found that a mood of 'happy determination' should prevail at this meeting, without it being heavy. Joining the course should be seen to be a serious undertaking, so the challenge to do regular link-work and attend regularly should not be underplayed, but a friendly atmosphere of mutual exploration should prevail. A little light-hearted banter is helpful, for those from outside the church may well expect long faces and solemnity.

Administrative arrangements should be carefully prepared – it shows that the leaders are careful and sensible. Uncertainty increases nervousness.

Someone from the church leadership should chair the meeting and introduce the other leaders. The following points should be made:

- The course is for beginners not experts. We will be starting at the beginning and will not be shocked by ignorance or questions about the existence of God and so on.
- During this nine-week course we shall look at the work of God our Father and how he sent his Son, Jesus, and the Holy Spirit into the world to make us whole. We shall not just be looking backwards at what happened 2,000 years ago, but at what these events mean for us today. We shall be seeing again and again how these can make a difference in our everyday lives. We shall also be looking for God to touch each of our lives in different ways and there will be times when we can open ourselves to him if we wish.
- The course demands commitment of a fairly high standard, in setting aside time for the meetings as an absolute priority, doing the link-work and being prepared actively to seek God.
- Each session will last for 90 minutes and there will always be a break after 90 minutes (for those who are being picked up or have to catch a bus).
- If someone wants to drop out of the course at any point that is fine. (Don't hassle them, but it would be helpful if they were to let you know so that you do not think they are ill.)
- Course members usually get to know one another quite well during a course, and this is one of its perks. However, it is quite

all right to come along and sit at the back and say nothing. There will be plenty of opportunities for asking questions.

- To allow free discussion it will be expected that all members will keep things they learn in the group about other people confidential – though what they learn about the Christian faith they can talk about with anyone!
- Members will need a copy of the link-work book, a notebook and a Bible.
- Arrange the date, place and time of at least the first three meetings. Suggest that members might like to help one another with transport. (This begins to build relationships and also helps those who will find actually getting to the first session a nerve-racking business, especially if it is held in a big house. A written reminder of time and place a few days before the first meeting will also help.)
- Ask the group to begin praying for one another and for the leaders between now and the beginning of the course. Remind them that they are not the only people feeling rather nervous.
- Any questions?

The course will probably be of more value if it follows a *Saints Alive! Life in the Spirit* course, or an Alpha course or similar.

▶ Informing the church

Make sure that your whole church congregation knows about the course and understands what is involved. The idea that this course is just for people who have a particular interest in healing, or that it is some sort of elitist gathering, needs to be firmly denied. The Christian healing ministry is recognised as an important part of the total pastoral work of the church in recent publications like *Common Worship – Pastoral Services* and the report *A Time to Heal*. This course should be seen as a means of introducing the idea of a healing ministry to a local church. Where such a ministry already exists it provides valuable ongoing training for those involved.

'Healing, we might say, is what the Church's mission is all about. Healing, wholeness, salvation – these words embrace what God has achieved for us through the incarnation of Jesus Christ. . .

The healing ministry in the parish is visionary . . . because it beckons us towards the future and a glimpse of the kingdom, the hope of creation renewed in perfect health and wholeness.

The healing ministry in the parish is prophetic . . . because it calls us to reconsider our relationship with God, each other and the world, and to seek forgiveness and a new start in our lives.

The healing ministry in the parish is dynamic . . . because Jesus is with us to the end of time: when we pray for his help, he comforts, strengthens and heals us, responding to our deepest need.'

(From the report *A Time to Heal*, Church House Publishing 2000)

1 What do we mean by 'healing'?

Aims

- To help group members settle into the course and get to know one another.
- To introduce the course, link-work books, etc.
- To broaden the group's understanding of healing and wholeness.

Outline and timing

It is very important that people feel relaxed and that their initial questions are answered, but at the same time you do need to get into the teaching of the course. Leaders will always need to be aware of the tension between the maintenance of the task and the care of the group.

All timings are only suggestions. Adapt the course to your needs. The refreshment break could come *after* the main teaching, in the middle of the session, rather than at the end.

0–20 mins	Getting started
	● Short opening prayer
	● Introduction and overview of the course
	● Distribute and explain the link-work books
20–50	Main learning focus: What do we mean by 'healing'?
	● Is healing an event or a process?
	● Group Bible study (Mark 5:21–34)
	● The process analysed
	● Healing and wholeness (*shalom*)
50–75	Ways of praying for healing (1)
	● Pray as you can, not as you can't

- Be specific
- Group prayer lists
75–90   Worship

Running Session 1

Preparation

- Pray for all those you expect to come, asking the Lord to protect them as they come to the meeting.
- Ensure that the meeting place is as comfortable as possible and that you have everything you need ready for the session: OHP, music for worship, Bibles, link-work books, etc.
- Prepare the Bible study on Mark 5:21–34.
- Photocopy an A4 sheet of paper for each member with the wholeness diagram and the lightning strike, but with no wording (see Appendix G).

The five tests

'It is my conviction that the Christian healing ministry (like every other form of ministry) should pass five tests of truth if it is to be acceptable.

1. It must be true to the Scriptures taken as a whole.
2. It must be true to what we know of Jesus.
3. It must be true to reason – because God gave us minds and presumably means us to use them.
4. It must be true to experience, and this must include personal experience, the experience of history and the traditional experience of the church.
5. It must be true to the prompting of the Holy Spirit in us.'
(Roy Lawrence, *The Practice of Christian Healing*, Triangle 1998)

Introductions

How personal introductions are made will depend upon the nature of the group. Often this course takes place as part of a church education programme, and as people already know one another introductions can be very brief. However, if several churches are coming together, or if there are new Christians present, the introductions may take longer. Try to keep them brief and suitable to the needs of your group.

Example of a formal introduction process

Each person says quite simply, 'My name is . . .' When they have all done this the leader reminds the group that we are all children of the same heavenly Father, and leads into the Lord's Prayer. (Make it quite clear which version you are going to use!) Or the leader might use the words of the 'Peace' – 'The peace of the Lord be always with you'.

Alternatively, your group may respond better to an 'icebreaker' – for example, divide people into pairs and give each person one minute to say why they have come on the course.

Overview of the course

This course should be seen as an introduction to the church's ministry of healing. It comprises nine sessions which are summarised in the Outline at the front of the link-work book.

Saints Alive! Healing in the Church is designed to give lay people confidence to pray for and with people who have problems and sickness. It may lead some people to make the Christian ministry of healing a main focus of their Christian witness.

(Note: Session 9 includes some material on how this basic course could be followed up and your church's policy on the Christian ministry of healing developed – or established if not already in place.)

Introducing the link-work books

Those people taking part in the course will need to purchase a copy of the link-work book. Go through the notes at the beginning of the link-work book. The format of daily Bible study has been changed slightly from previous editions.

The first five days of each week are allocated short Bible studies. Material on day 4 is to be used as an aid to contemplative prayer, and suggestions about how to use these verses are contained in the link-work book. Days 6 and 7 are allocated a 'chunk reading'. A summary of the teaching in each session is now also included in the link-work books.

Introductory prayer

Remember, this is a new group. If you feel that you ought to start with a prayer time it should be very short, committing the evening to God and possibly using a few well-known prayers. Avoid a dead formality, and keep it brief – there will be time for further prayer at the end of the evening.

▶ What do we mean by 'healing'?

Is healing an event or a process?

Group discussion

→ Briefly outline the story of a person who has appendicitis, under-goes a successful operation and makes a full recovery. Ask group members to buzz in pairs about the question 'When did healing take place?'

● At the onset of pain?
● When the correct diagnosis was made?
● During the successful operation?
● During the recovery period?

Now ask the group to imagine a person coming to a healing service, receiving prayer with the laying on of hands, and experi-encing a dramatic, visible healing. Ask members again to buzz in pairs on 'When did the healing take place?'

● When the person decided to seek relief from suffering?
● When the laying on of hands took place?
● As they accepted what happened?
● As they gave thanks for what happened?
● As they started a new life free from the suffering they had previ-ously known?

Group Bible study

➔ Read Mark 5:21–34. Make a list of the stages in the process of seeking healing undertaken by the woman with the issue of blood. Consider her faith, her perseverance, her desperation and her costly approach to Jesus.

Process mentality

It is important that we have a 'process mentality' about healing rather than an 'event mentality'. An event mentality leads us to look for instant answers to our problems, with inevitable disappointment when we do not usually see such answers. In the healing process, there may be specific events which stand out (eg the actual appendix operation), but they are all part of the process.

Christian healing and our relationship with Jesus

In many Gospel accounts of healing this process is evident and often ends with the sick person entering into a deep, personal relationship with Jesus. Thus the blind man in John 9 is sought out by Jesus after he is healed and John records that the man said, ' "Lord, I believe," and he worshipped him' (John 9:38). The woman in Mark 5 is not simply allowed to touch the hem of Jesus' garment and then go on her way. She is brought to a point where she has to relate to Jesus (Mark 5:33).

At a time when alternative and complementary therapies abound, it is important to stress that a relationship with Jesus is the unique element fundamental to our understanding of the Christian ministry of healing.

Group sharing

'Healing is Jesus Christ meeting us at our point of need.'
(Bishop Morris Maddocks)
'The Christian ministry of healing is more about relationship than remedy.'
(Author)

→ Invite any members of the group who wish, to briefly tell about their own experiences of Jesus meeting them at a point of need.

Hopes and fears (optional section)

This may also be a moment to invite the group to share any personal hopes and fears that they may have for the course, and any questions that are uppermost in their mind. For example, why does an all loving, all powerful God allow suffering? And if some are healed through our prayers why not everyone?

You won't be able to answer these questions fully now, but make a note of them and tell members that these and many other questions will be faced as the course proceeds, particularly in Session 4, 'Faith when things get tough', and Session 7, 'God and the mystery of suffering'.

▶ The healing process analysed

(See OHP 1)

1. Discovery. We discover that something is wrong. There are various signs – pain, weakness, the discovery of a lump, etc.
2. Admitting. We have to admit to ourselves, and then probably to others (eg a doctor), that there is something wrong.
3. Accepting help. If the problem is serious we shall have to accept help – maybe surgery, or a course of treatment. We actually have to accept this treatment – it is no good just thinking about it.
4. New lifestyle. If we are to benefit from the treatment we may have to adopt a new lifestyle. A person who discovers that he or she has diabetes may have to live with injections, and will certainly have to reduce their sugar intake.

> 'Jesus said to them, "It is not the healthy who need a doctor, but the sick. I have not come to call the righteous, but sinners."'
>
> (Mark 2:17)

The words 'heal' and 'save' in the New Testament both come from the same Greek root (*sozo*). How does the healing process compare with the process of personal salvation and sanctification, where we have to admit something is wrong, confess it, ask for God's grace and start living a new life in Christ?

See *The Christian Healing Ministry* by Morris Maddocks (SPCK 1995, chapter 3) for a detailed summary of biblical words used to describe healing. Speaking of *sozo* – to preserve, keep from harm, save from death, Maddocks writes: 'This verb is found more than a hundred times in the New Testament, and is used fourteen times in the Gospels in the sense to "make whole" in connection with Jesus' miracles of healing. On these occasions the double entendre of save/heal is never far from the surface.'

Optional group discussion
➔ When you come to God to confess your sins do you come thinking of God as
  ● a judge?
  ● a physician of your soul?
  ● a loving Father?
(People often see sin in terms of law-breaking and it is sometimes quite a revelation for them to see sin in terms of sickness. Of course, not all sickness is caused by sin.)

▶ Healing and wholeness
Brief introduction

Healing for the individual brings well-being, harmony, peace, joy and faith, as well as physical, emotional and spiritual health.

The biblical understanding may be summed up in the word 'wholeness', and healing might be described as a growth or transformation into wholeness. When we understand that, then we can see that:

- we are all in need of healing;
- healing is a life-long process involving many healing events.

John Donne wrote, 'No man is an island.' We live in a community with other women and men. We live in this world and relate to our environment. It is fundamental to our nature to want to relate to a being who is both beyond us and yet infinitely close to us – God. Healing and wholeness are not only about harmony within us, but about harmony outside us as well. We can express it in the following diagram.

The wholeness diagram

This circular diagram should be prepared in advance. It can either be drawn on a large circle of card or paper, or you could use OHP acetates (see Appendix G).

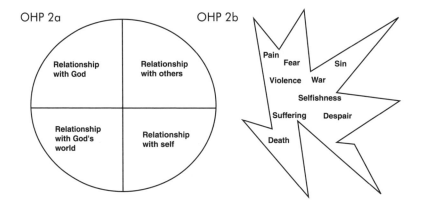

Teaching from the wholeness diagram

One area in which we all face problems is that of relationships. We may feel that we are square pegs in round holes, or that we are the only people in step! We also have problems in relating to nature – ask any gardener! Our aim here is to show that wholeness is about the totality of our life. Mental, physical and spiritual well-being are essential parts of this wholeness (1 Thessalonians 5:23).

A Hebrew word which encompasses the breadth of what we mean by healing and wholeness is *shalom*. It is usually translated as 'peace' but it has a much richer and broader meaning, including harmony of relationships, integrity of body, mind and spirit and good relationships within family and community. This is God's gift and cannot be earned. We see this *shalom* exemplified in Jesus, and he, of course, continually gave it to others: 'Peace I leave with you; my peace I give you' (John 14:27).

Group activity
→ Show the group the wholeness diagram (OHP 2a). Ask people to discuss in the full group how they see their relationship with God, God's world, themselves and others. When they have talked about this for a while, ask if their experience reflects the smooth, circular wholeness diagram. Discuss how Jesus gives us a model of perfect wholeness.

Very briefly look at Genesis 2:4–3:24. Adam and Eve enjoyed harmony – with God, with themselves and their personal sense of well-being, and with nature. All are affected by the Fall. (Avoid a sterile debate about whether Genesis is literal history: the important thing is that it teaches us the truth about the breakdown of all essential harmonious relationships.)

Now is the time to introduce the fragmentation diagram (OHP 2b). Place the lightning strike, with the words 'pain', 'sickness', 'war', etc., over the rounded wholeness circle. The circle now looks very different, with the picture fragmented and distorted. This is a more accurate representation of our experience, both as individuals and corporately. It is a picture of the fragmentation caused by the Fall. The healing ministry of Christ deals with the devastation of this fragmentation.

If you have prepared individual pieces of paper with the lightning strike, you could ask the group to fill in their own words on their own personal lightning strike, and after a few minutes share their findings in pairs.

▶ Ways of praying for healing (1)

Pray as you can, not as you can't

It is always tempting to look sideways at how other people pray and try to imitate them. This is a particular temptation when we are ministering alongside others, especially those who have more experience in praying for people in need than we have. There is nothing wrong with learning from others when the Holy Spirit prompts us. The problem is that we may be tempted to see prayer in terms of techniques.

Our prayer for others should grow out of a deepening relationship with God. *He* must guide us, and striving to pray in ways that are not true to ourselves is not helpful. (Acts 19:13–16 gives us a salutary example of people who tried to copy what the apostles were doing in the ministry of deliverance, without having the same relationship with Jesus.)

God is leading the whole church forward in the healing ministry, and insights about praying for others are being discovered and rediscovered all the time. It is quite appropriate for us to investigate these and to ask ourselves the question, 'Is this a way of praying which God wants me to make my own?'

Be specific

Jesus wants us to be real, and part of being real is being specific. Have a look at the healing of the blind beggar in Luke 18:35–43. Jesus asks him to be specific: *'What do you want me to do for you?'* If you listen carefully to the needs of the person who has come to you for prayer you should gain some understanding about their specific needs. (See Session 3 for brief introduction to listening skills.)

Group prayer lists

Explain to the group that you are going to draw up a group intercession list. Invite each member of the group to name a person who needs God's healing grace at this time. (This can only work with a group of under twelve people. If you are working with a much larger group it would be sensible to break the group down into several smaller groups of about seven people.)

Group work

→ Get the group members to write the names on the list at the beginning of the link-work books and ask the group to remember these people in their prayers. If possible they should write down specific requests, eg 'John – for freedom from pain, and a new knowledge of Jesus as his Lord and Saviour'. Or 'Jane – for safe outcome from her operation and complete recovery'. Remember – pray as you can, not as you can't!

Each week, ask how the people you are praying for are progressing. As the group begins to see answers to their prayers they will become enthused for this ministry. Encourage group members to pray aloud for those they have named during the prayer time in the final act of worship. This may well be a new experience for some. Teach them to use simple phrases like 'Jesus, we hold John in our prayers to you'. Give very clear instructions and keep the intercession time simple.

> 'Intercession is being in the presence of God with the people on your heart.'
>
> (Michael Ramsay)

▶ Worship and prayer

This act of worship should be kept simple. It is designed to make people feel at home in the group and encourage them to vocalise their prayers.

- A well-known hymn of praise (eg 'Praise, my soul' or 'Majesty').
- Bible reading (1 Timothy 2:1–8).
- The leader offers a short prayer for healing, then adds a phrase like 'We now mention by name those whom we feel the Holy Spirit has led us to pray for particularly at this time'.
- A quiet spiritual song.
- The grace (2 Corinthians 13:14, adapting 'you' to 'us').

For the next session, you may wish to pass the leadership of the prayers round the group. If so, ask people before they leave, and make sure they know what they are expected to do. (You will need to look ahead to Session 2 to see the suggested format of the prayers, or decide in advance your own order of worship.)

Resources for Session 1

- OHP diagrams for this session
  - OHP 1   Summary of the process from sickness to health
  - OHP 2a The wholeness diagram
  - OHP 2b The fragmentation overlay (overlay on 2a)
- Healing and wholeness source material:
  - Francis MacNutt, *Healing*, Ave Maria Press 1974, revised by Hodder 1997 (see chapters 4 and 11).
  - John Wimber, *Power Healing*, Hodder and Stoughton 1986 (see chapter 4, 'Healing the whole person').
  - Morris Maddocks, *The Christian Healing Ministry*, SPCK 1995 (see chapter 1, 'Healing and wholeness').

2 The healing ministry of Jesus (Part 1)

Aims

- To review the group's progress so far.
- To help the group see how Jesus dealt with each person in a unique way.

Outline and timing

0–20 mins	Getting started
	• Opening worship
20–40	Main learning focus: The healing ministry of Jesus (Part 1)
	• Knowing Jesus the healer
	• Bible study (Mark 2:1–12)
	• An overview of the variety of ways Jesus prayed for healing
40–60	Four basic kinds of healing:
	• Physical
	• Emotional
	• Relational
	• Deliverance
60–80	Ways of praying for healing (2)
	• The laying on of hands with prayer
80–90	Worship and prayer

▶▶ Running Session 2

Preparation

- Pray for all those you expect to come, asking the Lord to protect them as they come to the meeting.
- Do the link-work yourself.
- Go through the material, deciding as far as you can how you will pace the session.

Opening worship

- A well-known hymn or spiritual song (eg, 'Jesus is King' or 'Jesus! The name high over all').
- Read Mark 2:1–12
- Prayer asking for the guidance of the Holy Spirit.
- Silence.
- A quiet, reflective hymn or spiritual song.

(Having this worship planned in advance gives a clear signal to the group that the leader knows what he or she is doing and this helps build confidence.)

Review session

Be very relaxed about this. Keep it informal, simply making sure that all three areas are covered:

- Progress with the link-work books.
- How the people you prayed for last time are getting on. This could lead into a time of prayer and thanksgiving.
- Any other personal matters.

If a member of the group shares something that you feel needs ministry you will have to decide how and when to deal with it. Bear in mind that prayer ministry to an individual in the group can give the person a sense that they have been taken seriously, but it may frighten others away from sharing. Beware of attention seekers. However, if you say something like, 'Let's remember to pray about that at the end of the session,' this may cause anxiety, and detract from the main aim of the session.

To respond by suggesting that the matter probably needs prayer ministry, and asking the person to see you, either after the meeting or privately in the future, is often the best course of action. However, beware of opting out of ministry because of your own personal fears!

▶ The healing ministry of Jesus (Part 1)
Knowing Jesus the healer

'A Christian can never discuss healing without having Jesus in mind.'   (Bishop Morris Maddocks)

The name Jesus comes from a Hebrew root meaning to save, to heal, to deliver, to bring release. We could say that Jesus *is* healing.

It is important to point out that as we start to look at Jesus, we are not doing so to discover techniques for the ministry of healing. We look at the healing stories in the life of Jesus to get to know Jesus better. However, as we do this we will be able to discern the general principles which governed his ministry. For example:

● Jesus' ministry was concerned with meeting people at their point of need.
● Jesus did not simply deal with symptoms but went to the cause of the sickness.
● Jesus was perfectly in tune with the will of his heavenly Father.

This last point is particularly clear in John's Gospel: 'I tell you the truth, the Son can do nothing by himself; he can do only what he sees his Father doing, because whatever the Father does the Son also does' (John 5:19). The whole life of Jesus depended upon his relationship with the Father. He therefore ministered with the authority and power which flowed from his obedience.

The disciples were taught to relate to God as 'Father' (Luke 11:2); they were to wait for 'power from on high' (Luke 24:49); and in the Great Commission of Jesus they were given his authority (Matthew 28:18). Our aim as we go through this course is to try to learn the lessons that the disciples learned and to apply them to our situation.

Group Bible study

→ Divide the group into pairs or small groups. Give each group one or more healing events in the life of Jesus. Ask them to list any particular emphasis of teaching that the story highlights. You may find that there is more than one emphasis in the story.

This exercise will help the group to see Jesus in action, and should demonstrate the fact that each event is unique. Remember, we don't study the healing miracles of Jesus to find out techniques, but to come to know the healer.

For example, in the healing of the paralytic (Mark 2:1–12) we see the following emphases:
● The link between the man's sin and sickness.
● The faith and perseverance of his friends.
● In the context of conflict stories, the cost of healing.
● The story reinforces Mark's initial claim that the gospel is about Jesus, the Son of God (Mark 1:1).

The pairs should report back to the whole group and write up their findings on a flip chart. Talk about the variety of ways that Jesus worked, and the unique way he dealt with each sick person.

For a list of all the healing stories in the Gospels see Appendix A, and at the back of the link-work books (Appendix B).

An overview of Jesus' healing ministry

● Jesus saw beneath the surface to the root cause of a person's disease. See the story of the paralysed man (Mark 2:1–12) and the man at the pool (John 5:1–15).
● Jesus desired a real relationship with the sick person. See the story of the man born blind (John 9), and the woman with the haemorrhage (Mark 5:21–34).
● Jesus recognised that physical sickness is sometimes caused by

Satan's activity. See the story of the crippled woman (Luke 13:10–17).
- Jesus' healing ministry was costly, and it brought him into conflict (Matthew 9:1–8). On occasions it was draining (Luke 8:46).
- Sometimes it was a very public ministry, and at others, private. Compare the healing of Peter's mother-in-law in Mark 1:29–31 with the ministry to the crowds in verses 32–34.
- Jesus made use of sacramental signs – particularly touch, but also spittle (Mark 7:31–45), mud (John 9:6) and oil (as used by the disciples in Mark 6:13).
- Healing sometimes included deliverance from evil spirits (Mark 5:1–20).
- Jesus' healing power was born of a perfect relationship with his heavenly Father. See the story of the raising of Lazarus (John 11:1–44).

▶ Four basic kinds of healing

Francis MacNutt, in his book *Healing*, talks of four basic kinds of healing, and then goes on to describe how to pray for each. The four are:

- Physical (for problems caused by disease, accidents, etc.).
- Emotional (for problems causing mental pain, and any illness needing the healing of memories).
- Relational – healing of the diseased spirit (for problems caused by a person being out of harmony with God).
- Deliverance (for problems caused by the powers of darkness).

There is very often an interaction between all four. For example, a woman in her sixties comes seeking prayer for arthritis. She wants physical healing but counselling reveals that the arthritis flared up about six months after the death of her husband. She needs to work through her feelings of bereavement (emotional healing). She also confesses that she feels great bitterness towards her husband's sister, who caused her husband much anguish during his life and who did not attend his funeral. Much of her anger is focused on this woman, causing bitterness and a disease of her spirit. She also confides that after her husband's death she went on several occasions to a spiritualist and since then has been plagued by voices (powers of darkness).

This fabricated example, or a real one from your own experience of a similar nature, will begin to show group members that prayer for healing can be fairly complex.

Optional material

The subject of the powers of darkness must be faced squarely if questions are asked about it at this stage. Point out that this whole area of ministry will be dealt with later in the course (Session 8), but you might want to cover the following points here.

● Some sickness seems to be caused by a direct onslaught of Satan and the powers of darkness (Luke 13:10ff).
● Jesus is totally victorious over Satan through his sacrificial death and mighty resurrection (cf. Colossians 2:13–15). We pray *from* a victory, not *for* one!
● We are under the power and the authority of Jesus, and it is because of this that we minister in his power and authority.
● We need to pay attention to the safeguards essential for this type of prayer. In particular:
  – Never minister on your own if you think the powers of darkness are involved.
  – Never minister in this area without seeking advice from those in authority in your church.
  – Always seek prayer support.

▶ Ways of praying for healing (2)

The laying on of hands with prayer

'The hands are ours but the power is his.'   (Unknown)

Touching a person can be done with good or ill intent. The recipient very quickly senses the underlying motivation of the touch. In the laying on of hands with prayer, the physical action is an outward and visible symbol of closeness, harmony and concern. It is also a vehicle for the healing power of God. The following should be noted:

- There is no magical or mystical property in our hands.
- The moment of physical contact is an outward and visible sign of the love and power of God coming to the person who is being prayed for.
- It should be in response to the prompting of the Holy Spirit, not simply as a matter of course, and should accompany our prayer.
- Some signs of the Spirit's power may come as a result of the laying on of hands, eg heat, tingling, or quivering, etc. We should see these signs as outward and visible demonstrations of the power of God at work in someone's life. Where such signs occur, the person should maintain their prayer until the signs stop. If the person being prayed with is standing, the power of the Holy Spirit may cause them to fall down ('resting in the Spirit'). It is important to mention that such outward signs will not always accompany our prayers, and we should not give up, or feel worried, if there are no outward signs.
- The formal laying of hands on a person's head may not always be right (it can feel oppressive). A hand on a shoulder, or an arm placed round the person may be a good alternative to the more formal approach.
- If the person is disabled and sitting it may be right to kneel in front of them and simply hold their hands. Be sensitive to the situation of the person for whom you are praying.
- Everything should be done decently and in order. Women should be present where women are receiving the laying on of hands, and men should help with the ministry to men.
- It can be helpful to touch the wounded part of the body where modesty permits. Some people may be gifted in actually knowing where the seat of pain is, and then lay hands on this part.
- Refer to the guidelines for good practice in Session 8. (See also *A Time to Heal*, pp. 247–248.)

It may be helpful to demonstrate various ways of laying on hands with prayer. The laying on of hands symbolises sympathy for the sick and troubled, and the acceptance of all sick or outcast people. It demonstrates the love of God in his church for the world, and conveys the power of the Holy Spirit to the person being prayed for.

Group activity

→ Demonstrate various ways of laying on hands with prayer with group members and get them to feed back how they 'feel'. Get the group to practise in groups of three, each taking it in turns to have hands laid on them with prayer. Our aim must be to communicate love and acceptance. Anything which takes away the 'patient's' sense of independence, or which seems dominating, should be avoided.

Get the group members to talk about their own experiences in this area.

(See OHP 3.) The laying on of hands should be used
- *with* prayer, care, others, gentleness, awareness, God's love and power;
- *without* being oppressive, dominating or abusive.

▶ Worship and prayer

The cost of healing

This time of worship should also include a Bible study on the theme of the cost of healing. Because healing seeks to re-establish harmony and wholeness in a fragmented situation, it is always costly (see Isaiah 53).

- Hymn (eg 'There is a Redeemer' or 'Lord Jesus Christ').
- Bible reading (Mark 5:1–20).
- Very briefly outline the ways in which this story points to the cost of healing:
  - (a) For the man possessed. (Note the conflict in coming to Jesus and yet not wanting a relationship with him.)
  - (b) For the owner of the pigs!
  - (c) For the villagers, who would have to accept the outcast back into their society.
  - (d) For Jesus, who took on the role of outcast and was sent away.

- Intercession and ministry (if it is felt appropriate).
- Final hymn or spiritual song.

These are only suggestions for the worship time. The meditation in Appendix B might be useful. However, such imaginative exercises depend very much upon the maturity of the group and the confidence of the leader. If the group comprises fairly new Christians then the straightforward Bible study on Mark 5:1–20 is to be recommended.

Preparation for next session

If you are using group members to lead worship, tell them now what you would like them to do in the next session.

 # Resources for Session 2

- OHP diagram for this session
  - OHP 3, The laying on of hands with prayer
- Laying on of hands with prayer source material:
  - John Richards, *The Question of Healing Services*, Daybreak 1989. Chapter 6 is a comprehensive introduction to the subject of the laying on of hands.
  - *A Time to Heal*, Church House Publishing 2000 (pp. 247–248).
  - Gerard W. Hughes, *God of Surprises*, Darton, Longman and Todd, 1996. There is an excellent treatment of the Mark 5:1–20 passage in chapter 3 on page 27, headed 'Inner chaos and false images of God'.

3 Approaches to healing – Christian and others

 **Aims**

- To set our understanding of the Christian ministry of healing in the context of the other approaches to healing today, both medical and spiritual.
- To help the group understand where the Lord is leading his church in this ministry at this time.

 Outline and timing

0–20 mins	Getting started
	● Review of progress so far, particularly with reference to the intercession lists
	● Opening worship
20–50	Main learning focus: the Christian ministry of healing in today's world
	● Healing and medicine
	● Various views of the Christian ministry of healing
	● Alternative therapies
	● Sickness and sin (optional section)
50–65	Ways of praying for healing (3)
	● An introduction to listening skills
	● 'Two-way' listening
65–90	Worship, intercession and ministry

▶▶ Running Session 3

Preparation

- Pray for all those you expect to come, asking the Lord to protect them as they come to the meeting.
- Pray against any spirit of confusion – particularly when you come to discuss alternative and complementary medicine today.
- Ask the Holy Spirit's help to be concise in teaching about healing and medicine and the various views of the Christian ministry of healing.
- Do the link-work yourself during the week.
- Have large sheets of paper and coloured markers for group work and for other notes or lists.

Opening worship

- A time of praise, perhaps including the songs 'Praise the name of Jesus' and 'Father, we adore you'.
- Report on the progress of those who are on the prayer list, noting where thanks should be given, and where you feel that prayer may need to be intensified or modified.
- Sum up this report-back in a time of prayer.
- A hymn or spiritual song.

Review session

Ideally the group is beginning to settle down and less time will be spent in going through the link-work and other personal matters. The suggestion to move the report-back about people on the prayer list into the opening worship section may not be right for every group, but it is done so that thanks and effective prayer can be made for them right at the beginning, and to keep the group looking outwards.

The comments about the most appropriate time for ministry (see notes for Session 2) still apply.

▶ The Christian ministry of healing in today's world

Healing and medicine

Quickly brainstorm and write down some answers to the question, 'What aspects of medical science have been most significant in combating sickness and disease?'

Medical science as practised today has brought help and healing to countless millions. Detailed observation of how our bodies work and what hinders health has led to advances in medical techniques and treatment far beyond anything anyone could have imagined. Emphasise that this is all part of God's healing work. Good medical practice will not only use direct treatment, but will also include health education, environmental and social issues, etc.

Human beings are a wonderful combination of body, mind and spirit, and medical science today is beginning to take seriously our need to deal with the spiritual as well as the physical and mental aspects of human nature.

> 'As man is body, mind and spirit, and health depends on the harmonious function of the whole man, so the tasks of medicine and the church are inseparable: co-operation thus comes into line with Christ's charge to his disciples to heal and preach.'
> (From the British Medical Association Committee report of 1956, 'Divine healing and the co-operation between doctors and clergy')

We must avoid making a false distinction between what is 'normal' and what is 'supernatural'. 'I am the Lord, who heals you' (Exodus 15:26) applies as much to healing through medicine as it does to answered prayer. In the Old Testament, various natural aids to healing are mentioned: wine, water, salt, oil, fruits, leaves, bandages, etc. Isaiah ordered a poultice of figs to be applied to Hezekiah's boil, and his life was spared (2 Kings 20:7).

> 'Honour the physician . . . he has been created by the Lord. The
> Lord uses physicians to heal and relieve pain . . . My son, when
> you are ill, do not be depressed, but pray to the Lord and he will
> heal you.'
>
>   (Ecclesiasticus 38:1, 7, 9 in the Apocrypha)

In the New Testament, Jesus used natural means like spittle and mud, and recommended food for Jairus's daughter, but clearly 'signs and wonders' accompanied his ministry as well.

We can therefore see clearly from Scripture that there are two major errors we need to avoid:

- We are not to confine healing to medical science only and deny the possibility of divine intervention. We believe in an incarnational God who loves us, and who is described as 'the Lord who heals'.
- We are not to see God acting only in what appear to be supernatural ways. This is a recipe for extremism and imbalance. It can lead to a refusal to accept medical intervention, causing unnecessary suffering and possibly even death. This does not honour God.

Group discussion
→ Allow the group to share any personal thoughts on this matter or stories of people who have been hurt by a false or narrow belief.

▶ Various views about the Christian ministry of healing

Start this section with a very brief outline of the way the Christian healing ministry has developed. The ministry of Jesus was shared with the apostles and disciples (Luke 9–10). The early church was filled with power and healed the sick in Acts 3. Sadly, for various reasons, the church's ministry of healing declined after this.

The various views of the Christian ministry of healing may be briefly summarised as follows. (See OHP 4.)

1. The 'booster rocket' view

This view sees the accounts of healing in the early church as a special 'booster' that God gave, which fell away after that initial surge of power. Healing in New Testament times is seen as a special dispensation. It is argued by some that there is much variety in the divine economy in the Bible, and that God has dealt differently with people in different eras of biblical history. The problem, of course, with this view is that it is not borne out by the facts. God's healing grace can be seen in evidence in every period of the church's history.

2. The 'saints and shrines' view

God's healing grace is poured out in modern times, but it is especially manifest at certain places like Walsingham and Lourdes, or through very special 'holy' people who are often designated 'saints'. While not wishing to decry the special ministry of certain individuals, or the tremendous blessing that pilgrimage to certain holy places has given to people, we must ask ourselves whether God's healing grace is limited in this way. Might an emphasis on 'saints and shrines' create a barrier to the belief that the healing grace of God can be poured out in any congregation at any time and at any place?

3. The 'sacramental' view

A sacrament has been described as an outward sign of an inward spiritual grace. The Christian healing ministry uses such signs. The laying on of hands with prayer, and anointing with oil are sacramental acts. Confession is being broadened to include healing of memories. The Eucharist, or Holy Communion, is the great healing sacrament, and many churches are now including a time for the ministry of healing in the context of eucharistic worship. This is good, but it can lead to a 'priestly and professional' approach to the ministry of healing.

4. The 'every-member ministry' view

This view takes seriously the fact that we are 'the body of Christ' (1 Corinthians 12:27). We are all called to ministry by virtue of our baptism. Every member of the body of Christ has a ministry of reconciliation, prayer, love and healing. This is often combined with the charismatic emphasis that we need the gifts and graces of God to fulfil this ministry. For us to fulfil this high calling we need to be 'clothed with power from on high' (Luke 24:49) 'when the Holy Spirit comes upon [us]' (Acts 1:8). While this view is often seen as a 'new' emphasis, it is in fact one which has been part of the church's experience down the ages.

5. The 'faith healing and psychic gifts' view

A widespread and growing view is that 'healing' can come as the result of people using psychic gifts, or some special method or power. Much New Age practice falls into this category. Jesus is often held up to be a good example of a person who uses such gifts, but his uniqueness as the Son of God, at whose name every knee shall bow, is denigrated. We must be very clear that the Christian ministry of healing is unique. Some psychic practices may be natural; others of occult origin. Occult practices are condemned in the Bible, and we must not allow our ministry to be contaminated in any way by them.

Group discussion
→ Which of these five views of Christian healing do you find helpful? (Note: it is possible to combine various views to some extent. For example, the sacramental view and the every-member ministry view may well be held satisfactorily in tension within a church.)

Alternative therapies

There is a whole range of alternative therapies which people use today outside of normal medical practice. Some common examples are:

- acupuncture
- aromatherapy
- reflexology
- homoeopathy
- iridology
- herbal medicine
- spiritist healing

These may present problems for those of us involved in the Christian ministry of healing.

First, in the minds of many people, Christian healing is lumped together with all these practices. The unique feature of Christian healing is that it should bring us into a living relationship with Jesus Christ as our Lord and Saviour. *We preach the gospel* and heal the sick.

Secondly, people may perceive any great signs and wonders accompanying the Christian ministry of healing as no different from what can be obtained through these alternative means.

And thirdly, some of these alternative methods are plainly condemned in Scripture and open people to demonic forces (eg spiritist healing).

We might well ask the following questions about any 'alternative therapy':

● Is it some sort of placebo?
● Is it part of the healing that God gives in creation which we may use?
● Is it relying on counterfeit powers, remembering that the devil is 'the prince of liars' and that the best lies mimic the truth. (Counterfeit bank notes are best when they are very close to the true ones!)

In ministering to people who have been involved in New Age and occult practices we should avoid:

● entering into a sterile debate about the nature of the alternative therapy which the person asking for prayer has been using;
● implying any criticism of the person involved as we seek to deal with the erroneous teaching of the therapy;
● frightening the person by speaking of demonic influence.

The following check list can be used to assess the exact nature of a complementary or alternative healing method.

A Christian approach to alternative medicine (OHP 5)

1. Is the method in line with biblical teaching?
2. Does the 'patient' come into any form of 'bondage' to the therapist?
3. Are the gullible exploited?
4. Are unconscious minds exposed to unknown powers and forces?
5. Is there any contact with spirits or any form of spiritism?
6. Does the 'healer' claim to have special healing powers?
7. Are unknown spiritual forces used?
8. Does the technique employ pseudo-scientific jargon or procedures?
9. Does the method produce a greater overall freedom and harmony for the client?
10. Do you have a sense of unease in any way about the method?

Group discussion
→ It is quite likely that there will be considerable discussion and sharing on this issue. Beware of confusion or getting hung up on one particular therapy. Remember that some people may have a 'hidden agenda' about one or other method of alternative medicine, but anyone genuinely searching for healing can come in prayer to Jesus Christ.

Sickness and sin (optional section)

Time constraints may mean that this section will need to be omitted. The leader should bear in mind that this material is here and if the question of sickness and sin and the relationship between them comes up in future, they can refer back to it.

When the Israelites settled down as a community, God gave them certain rules for public health and hygiene (eg Leviticus 11–15). There was a strong awareness of the corporate responsibility for the health of the community. Rules about food, infectious diseases and damp housing were all carefully spelled out, as were many other matters concerning cleanliness and public health. (Note how there is a parallel between infectious skin diseases and diseases of the fabric of home, eg mildew and dry rot.)

There were three spin-offs from this:

- The power of the professional priesthood, who acted as public officers of health.
- An inexorable link between sickness and sin – if you were sick it was because in some way or other you had sinned, or broken the rules.
- The inevitable isolation of the sick as a public health precaution (eg special colonies for lepers). Note too how the sin-bearing animal was driven out from the community into the wilderness carrying with it the sins of the community (Leviticus 16:21–22).

Group discussion

→ Discuss together how widespread you think the idea is today that sickness is often caused by sin. And how should we respond to the person who says, 'I don't know what I have done to deserve this'?

Look at the following three stories, noting particularly what Jesus says about the relationship between sin and sickness in each one:
- Mark 2:1–12   The healing of the paralytic
- John 9:1–41   The man born blind
- John 5:1–14   The invalid at the pool

▶ Ways of praying for healing (3)

Developing listening skills

Being able to listen effectively is crucial in any healing ministry. A whole course could be devoted to listening skills. Members of the group may find it useful to obtain the Grove booklet *The Wisdom to Listen* by Michael Mitton.

Note 1. The word counselling has today taken on a narrow, professional context. While some group members may go on to take specific counselling courses and gain academic recognition for this, this course is concerned with lay people involved in a prayer ministry for those who come to them, under the authority and supervision of the local church. Maybe we should try to adopt a term like 'Christian befriender' rather than 'counsellor', so that it is quite clear that we are not claiming any professional status in this ministry.

Note 2. The Acorn Trust has developed a network of courses under trained tutors called 'Christian Listeners'. This would provide a good follow-on for those who wish to look in more detail at this subject of how to listen well.

Group discussion
→ 'Making space for people is a healing activity' (Angela Ashwin) and listening to people is a vital ingredient in this. Discuss ways in which we can 'make space' for people.

> 'Then they sat on the ground with him for seven days and seven nights. No-one said a word to him, because they saw how great his suffering was.'
>
> (Job 2:13)

Whatever we may think of the subsequent advice given by Job's comforters, they started along the right lines by sitting and empathising with the tormented Job for as long as was necessary.

Reflecting back what a person has said

This is a very important skill associated with listening. From time to time the listener will summarise the essential elements of what he or she has just heard. This:

● assures the person that he or she is being listened to carefully;
● helps to clarify the real issues being shared;
● builds up an atmosphere of trust.

For example, a person has come for prayer because he or she is claustrophobic. The person vividly remembers being shut in a loft when very young, and for ten minutes will describe painfully what happened. You may respond by saying, 'Suddenly hearing the door of the loft close and finding yourself alone in the darkness was obviously a terrifying experience. I feel that it has taken a lot out of you to tell me about it, but that it was also a relief to share it. Are there any other episodes from your childhood which you feel you would like to talk through?'

In this illustration the listener has:

- summarised very briefly the content of the person's story;
- shown an understanding that the person is feeling vulnerable;
- gently led the person on to other episodes.

This process may need to be repeated several times in the course of an interview. It is important to stress that it is not the role of the listener to make value judgements. In the above example it would have been very unhelpful to say, 'Perhaps with hindsight you can see it was silly to get frightened.'

Mention the importance of eye contact, and observing not only what the person says but also their body language, which may indicate what is going on beneath the surface.

Group activity

→ In pairs, get people to tell one another about an incident which is very vivid to them. The partner listens, saying nothing, and then reflects back in a very few words:
- the incident the person has described;
- the emotions that were felt.

They then exchange roles and repeat the exercise. Return to the full group to reflect upon the activity.

Remember the aim is to pray effectively for people. Some people are just attention-seeking and will not really want to move on to prayer.

Or they may have a deep fear of being prayed for. Listening to people is, as Angela Ashwin says, a healing activity, but prayer opens the person to the healing touch of the Holy Spirit. Listen by all means, and listen well, but do not allow prayer to be cut short because of the time spent listening.

> 'Don't use prayer as an escape from the pain of listening, or the need to listen as an escape from the challenge of praying!'

Two-way listening

Encourage the group members to learn to listen to God. The link-work readings also carry on this theme. Discuss the ways in which God speaks to us – gifts of knowledge, through quiet meditation on his word, through the inner, still small voice, and so on. Suggest to the group members that they need to cultivate two-way listening. They should be asking the following two questions in any interview or talk with a person seeking healing:

- What is the person really trying to say?
- Is the Holy Spirit speaking to me about this situation?

If we do not get gifts of knowledge on every occasion, this is an encouraging not a discouraging sign. It helps to show us that we are not just making things up. Encourage members to act on the words that they believe might be from God.

The atmosphere surrounding a healing in the Gospels was in some cases important. For example, Jesus took the deaf and dumb man away from the noisy crowd (Mark 7:32 ff), and on one occasion the atmosphere of unbelief meant that the ministry of Jesus was in some way limited (Mark 6:5). You should aim at an atmosphere of quiet acceptance of God's presence and his love.

▶ Worship and prayer

- Hymn or song.
- Intercessions.

Use a Scripture verse such as Matthew 4:24 and then pray for each person on the group's list and others, perhaps like this:

Leader: 'Lord Jesus we bring to you John for healing after his heart attack.'

Everyone: 'The people brought to him all who were ill with various diseases . . . and he healed them.'

Leader: 'Lord Jesus we pray that Mary will be relieved from the pain.'

Everyone: 'The people brought to him all who were ill with various diseases . . . and he healed them.'

This 'litany' approach firmly links our intercessions with the Jesus of the Gospels, and reminds us that true healing comes when a person is united to Jesus.

- A time of ministry, if appropriate.
- A time of thanksgiving.
- Final hymn (eg 'Father, I place into your hands').

Preparation for next session

If you are using group members to lead the worship, tell them now what you would like them to do in the next session. Inform the group that next week you will look at the place of faith in the healing ministry of Jesus and his church.

Resources for Session 3

- OHP diagrams for this session
  - OHP 4, Views about healing
  - OHP 5, Alternative medicine – a Christ – approach
- Listening skills source material:
  - Michael Mitton, *The Wisdom to Listen*, a Grove booklet which you might consider buying for every member of the group.
  - Joyce Huggett, *Listening to God* (1986), and *Listening to Others* (1988), Hodder and Stoughton.
  - Colin Urquhart, *Receive Your Healing*, Hodder and Stoughton 1986 (particularly chapters 38–40).
  - Angela Ashwin, *Heaven in Ordinary*, Mayhew McCrimmon

1985. This is a most valuable little book, which might be offered for sale to group members.
- John Wimber, *Power Healing*, Hodder and Stoughton 1986. (Appendix A – The Old Testament, Appendix B – The healing ministry of Jesus, and Appendix C – The healing ministry of the disciples.)

4 The part played by faith

Aim

- To explore what we mean by 'faith', and to discover the part faith played in the healing ministry of Jesus.

 Outline and timing

Consider placing the refreshment break between part one and part two of the main teaching.

0–20 mins	Getting started
	● Questions raised by the course so far
	● Other feedback
	● Opening worship
20–45	Main learning focus: The part played by faith
	● Introduction and group activity
	● Faith and the ministry of Jesus
	● The 'visibility' of faith
	● The effect of faithlessness (optional)

Optional refreshment break

45–60	Part played by faith (continued)
	● Faith when things get tough
70–80	Ways of praying for healing (4)
	● Building up our faith
	● Dealing with doubts
80–90	Thanksgiving and praise

▶ Running Session 4

Preparation

- Pray for all those who expect to come, asking the Lord to protect them as they come to the meeting.
- Have a large scarf ready for the blindfold activity.
- Have large sheets of paper and coloured markers for group work and for other notes or lists.

General notes

The question of faith is central to our understanding of Christian healing, but it can also cause great misunderstanding. People talk about 'faith healing', and this can cover many approaches to healing, including occult and mediumistic methods which are not biblical.

When prayer is offered and the person does not get well, people can feel threatened and say that the cause was a lack of faith. This adds a sense of guilt to an already difficult situation.

Some people see faith as being able to assent to articles of Christian belief. The slightest question over a clause of the Creed can cause such people to feel that they have no faith. You need to be aware of these and other misconceptions. Much will be gained by letting people share where they are in their understanding of faith. Remind them of the definition of faith in Hebrews: 'Faith is being sure of what we hope for and certain of what we do not see' (Hebrews 11:1).

The main aim of this session is to show that faith is about a trust in a living and loving God, and that this trust is made visible as we step out in action.

The question of faithlessness and its effect is important, but it has been made optional because it will probably have come up in discussion at some point during the session.

▶ The part played by faith

Brief introduction

Keep this summary very brief. There are four types of faith in the New Testament. Outline these very quickly.

1. Faith as a basic trust in God (Hebrews 11:6).
2. Faith which is a credal statement.
3. Faith which is a gift of God (1 Corinthians 12:9).
4. Faithfulness which is part of the fruit of the Holy Spirit (Galatians 5:22).

The first of these is fundamental. It grows as we discover the character of God, as revealed in his word and checked in the light of our own experience. We need to know God and to have faith in God (2 Chronicles 20:20; Mark 11:22) not faith in our faith.

> 'I do not have great faith, but I have faith in a great God.'
> (Corrie Ten Boom)

Such faith can be summarised in the phrase 'I believe and trust in him'. Both elements are needed. I might believe that a friend can drive a car, but that is not the same as trusting myself in the front passenger seat!

Group activity
➔ Try this as a fun way to demonstrate faith and trust.

One member of the group is taken outside the room and blindfolded. A simple 'obstacle course' is set up in the room. A member of the group is chosen to guide the blindfolded person round the obstacle course. This should be done if possible without touching the blindfolded person. A calm, quiet, reassuring, affirming approach will get the best results! The two people then share with the group their feelings.

Draw out from them lessons about faith:
- Did faith grow and develop as the task progressed?
- Which of the two people felt they were taking risks?
- Did love or concern develop during the exercise?

Ask the group to discuss how they think this example illuminates their understanding of faith.

Note: It would be possible to start the whole evening off with this exercise, particularly if you feel the group is getting locked into formality by following the same pattern each week. Try to choose a calm type of person to be blindfolded! Remember that this activity can raise anxieties. There follows an additional or alternative group activity.

Alternative group activity

→ Get people to call out the sort of people we have to trust, eg an airline pilot, an anaesthetist, a car driver, etc. Invite one or two members of the group to share very briefly a time when they had to trust someone absolutely. What were their feelings?

A Methodist evangelist, Sam P. Jones, preached a sermon in May 1885 seeking to help people who were continually praying for more faith. He encouraged them to start to act on their faith. 'Faith is only evidenced by action,' he said. In the same sermon he used the phrase 'Faith is spelt RISK', a phrase later made famous by John Wimber. Encourage a short discussion on this phrase and whether people agree with it.

Faith and the ministry of Jesus

In the ministry of Jesus we see faith operating in different people:

- Faith of the sufferer. See, for example, Mark 5:21–34, the woman with the issue of blood.
- Faith of the intermediary – in the person or persons seeking healing for a friend or relative. See, for example, Mark 5:21–43, Jairus coming in faith to Jesus for his daughter.
- Faith of the intercessor – the faith of those who pray for the sick.

It is worth noting that Jesus reserved some of his harshest criticism for those who pray but have no faith: 'O unbelieving generation . . .' (Mark 9:19).

● The faith of the Saviour – the faith of Jesus himself. Hebrews 12:2 speaks of Jesus as 'the author and perfecter of our faith'.

The faith of Jesus is always present. In a particular situation the faith of the sufferer or the intercessor may be added.

> 'I tell you the truth, anyone who has faith in me will do what I have been doing. He will do even greater things than these because I am going to the Father.'
>
> (John 14:12)

The visibility of faith

There are several occasions, both in the Gospels and in the Acts of the Apostles, where the faith of people is visible. Faith is made visible through obedience. St Thomas Aquinas said, 'It is God who causes faith in the believer by *prompting his will* and enlightening his intellect' (italics mine). Thus the blind man in John 9 obeys when Jesus tells him to go and wash in the pool of Siloam (John 9:1–7).

Group discussion

→ Who shows faith in each of the following examples? How can that faith be seen?

● Mark 2:5
● Mark 5:34
● Luke 7:9
● Luke 17:19
● Luke 18:42
● Acts 14:9–10

Our interior faith is demonstrated by our actions (James 2:14–26).

Group discussion (optional)

→ Divide into sub-groups of two or three and share any personal accounts of times when faith has been made visible.

Group role discussions (optional)

→ A new member of your church comes for prayer for the first time, asking the question, 'Do I have to have faith before God can heal me?' How will you answer?

The effect of faithlessness (optional section)

Lack of faith can block God's love acting in our lives: 'He could not do any miracles there, except lay his hands on a few sick people and heal them. And he was amazed at their lack of faith' (Mark 6:5–6). Jesus was aware that lack of belief could block healing. Earlier in Mark's Gospel Jesus had encouraged the synagogue ruler with the words, 'Don't be afraid, just believe' (Mark 5:36). He 'put out' all the people who were weeping and wailing, and took only those who had faith into the room with him.

> 'The true antidote to fear is not courage but faith.'
>
> (Unknown)

The gift of faith (1 Corinthians 12:9)

A gift of faith is a deep and overwhelming conviction that God will act in a specific way in a particular situation. Many examples are seen in the life of Jesus, especially in John 11 (the raising of Lazarus). A person might receive a very clear instruction from the Lord like 'anoint her eyes', and therefore they *know* that this is his ministry. Sometimes such faith is accompanied by other gifts of the Holy Spirit, like the gift of knowledge. Someone may 'know' what is wrong, or where the pain is, and this gives rise to deep, inner knowledge that once again God is in control of this ministry. Some people have pictures in their mind that give them this surge of faith. For example, when ministering to a person who has a deformity, they may 'see' the person perfectly whole and so can pray that into reality.

There can be a danger of wishful thinking being confused with a gift of faith. This is particularly common where close relatives are involved in ministry. Naturally their deepest desire is the health of the loved one, and this can become so intense that it is mistaken for a gift of faith. Some clergy starting out in the ministry of healing have been mistaken about a gift of faith because they were motivated by a strong desire to see the healing ministry progress in their parish.

But having mentioned the negative things, it is also wise to emphasise that it is the experience of many Christians that, when they have stepped out in faith, time and time again God has honoured their prayer. Continual use of the gift of faith builds up faith in us.

Group discussion

→ Share in the group any times when members have felt their expectation that God was going to act was informed by a gift of faith. Make a list of these. In the discussion you will probably encounter some of the problems that people have when given gifts of faith.

Group role discussion (optional)

→ A member of your church comes for prayer stating that they have absolute faith that God is going to heal them. How do you respond?

Gifts of faith often push us into actions that we would not normally contemplate, and we shall have to deal with our human reactions.

- Doubt ('Am I making this up?')
- Fear ('I might look a complete fool!')
- Sin (unwillingness to obey)

We may worry that we have not discerned God's will properly. How can this self-doubt be overcome? (See the section on ways of praying for healing below.) What are the appropriate actions that we should take if we do get something wrong?

For example, as a result of what you thought was a gift of faith you have prayed for a poorly sighted person to see clearly. You have encouraged the person to build up hope that this will happen. Nothing seems to have changed. What should you do?

- Admit that you were wrong and, if you feel this is appropriate, apologise.
- Maintain a close relationship with the person; it is very tempting to run away from the situation.
- Talk through the whole matter with them when it is right to do so.
- When you get another possible gift of faith step out again. Don't let the former experience stop you going on in this ministry!
- Ensure that you have someone who is able to 'supervise' your ministry. (See Session 8 on guidelines for good practice.)

▶ Faith when things get tough

When we are faced with a particularly difficult situation (for example, praying for a young person who seems to be getting steadily worse from a life threatening condition and all the signs point to a premature death) what can we do to maintain faith?

- Look at Jesus, not at the problem (Hebrews 12:2). (See Matthew 14:22–36, especially verse 30.)
- Sometimes we will need to wrestle with God in prayer for these sorts of conditions. (See Genesis 32:22–31.)
- We need to rely on one another for support in such times. (See Galatians 5:6b and 6:2.)

In the Garden of Gethsemane Jesus subtly changed his prayer as the time of his arrest came closer. He started by praying, 'My Father, if it is possible, may this cup be taken from me. Yet not as I will, but as you will' (Matthew 26:39). Then this changes to 'My Father, if it is *not* possible for this cup to be taken away unless I drink it, may your will be done' (Matthew 26:42). The negative 'not' is carefully inserted in the Greek, and it would seem that Matthew is stressing that, as the prayer proceeds, the emphasis is modified.

As we move on in prayer in these tough circumstances we may find our emphasis changes, but hopefully never our trust in our loving Father. This is not the same as simply 'copping out' as soon as the going gets tough.

Our ultimate belief must be that God loves us and desires our well-being. This is shown clearly by what Jesus did for us on the cross. We hang on to this truth on our life's journey. Sometimes life gets so tough that it is like an overhang on a cliff, and we have to trust ourselves to this 'rope' of faith. But always in the Christian life we travel together and rely on one another for support over the difficult bits.

(See OHP 6, Faith when things get tough.)

▶ Ways of praying for healing (4)

Building up our faith

It is important to pray within our faith. God is not honoured if we pray for healing when we are not able to believe that God will heal in a situation. There are many pressures which may force us to pray beyond our faith.

- Group pressure. What will people think if we do not seem to have faith for healing in this situation?
- The desire to convince God that we do really believe he can heal in the situation!
- Sheer desperation, particularly if the sick person is a dearly loved friend or family member.

We must pray within our faith, and when we see answers to prayer, use them to build up our faith. For example, our initial prayer for a person severely disabled with arthritis might be that just one finger could be freed. When we see this happen we are then given faith to believe that God is at work and so our faith is built up. We can then pray for further healing.

Dealing with our doubts

- We should confess our doubts to the Lord ('I do believe; help me overcome my unbelief!' – Mark 9:24). It is important that we accept his loving forgiveness.
- Look at the Lord and not at the problem (Matthew 14:22–32; Hebrews 12:2).

- Read faith-building books or listen to faith-building tapes. These often contain remarkable testimonies of God's loving intervention.
- Ask for help, ministry and support from other Christians. Pride tells us to try to get through it in our own strength; humility seeks help and befriending.

▶ Worship and prayer

- A time of thanksgiving for the gifts of faith that people have experienced.
- A time of confession and ministry for people who feel that they have problems with their faith.
- A final act of praise to our God who is faithful (eg 'Great is thy faithfulness').

■ Resources for Session 4

- OHP diagram for this session;
  - OHP 6, Faith when things get tough
- The part played by faith source material:
  - Francis MacNutt, *Healing*, Hodder 1997. See particularly chapters 8 and 9, 'Faith to be healed' and 'The mystery of faith'.
  - Francis MacNutt, *The Power to Heal*, Ave Maria Press 1977. See particulary chapters 3 and 4, which deal with soaking prayer and degrees of improvement.
  - Francis MacNutt, *The Prayer that Heals*, Hodder 1991.
  - John Gunstone, *Prayers for Healing*, Highland 1988.

5 The healing ministry of Jesus (Part 2)

Aims

- To explore how Jesus balanced love and power in his ministry.
- To consider his claim that healing is a sign of the kingdom.
- To introduce the idea that Jesus' aim was to share his ministry with others.

Outline and timing

0–15 mins	Getting started
	● Review of progress
	● Opening worship
15–40	Main learning focus: The healing ministry of Jesus (Part 2)
	● The balance between proclamation and demonstration
	● The balance between love and power
	● The ministry of healing as a sign of the kingdom
40–60	Beginning to look at our own ministry
	● Hopes and fears
	● The questionnaire
60–80	Ways of praying for healing (5)
	● Using the gift of tongues
80–90	Worship, prayer and ministry

Running Session 5

In this session we introduce the idea that we are called to share in the healing ministry of Jesus. For some this will be nothing new, but for others it may well be very challenging. In order to introduce the concept gradually but firmly, the next three sessions contain progressive steps in this process.

This session gives some scriptural background, concentrating on the concept of healing as a sign of the kingdom of God and the balance between love and power. Time is given to examining how people are feeling about the possibility of a healing ministry. At the mid-point in this session the questionnaire in Appendix A of the link-work books is introduced. Course members are asked to complete this in order to discover where they are in their thinking and experience.

The sixth session will go over some of the basic teaching about being filled with the power of the Holy Spirit, which leaves the final three sessions to tackle some of the difficult questions raised by this ministry, and to point the way forward.

Preparation

Pray especially that members of the group will begin to catch the vision that they can be involved in Christ's ministry of healing, and that they will be excited and enthused to go forward in this ministry.

Review of progress

Spend time at the beginning of this session asking how people feel about the course so far. Ask all the group members to give the group an update of the people they put on the prayer list. This is very important at this stage; it is easy to lose sight of the fact that one essential part of this course is ongoing prayer for sick people. Our enthusiasm to move on to the main learning focus of the week must not cause the intercession list to be neglected.

Opening worship

By now you will have settled into some form of opening worship which suits the group. Maybe this is the week to introduce something a little different. You might like to consider using Taizé music, some acts of worship from the Iona Community or other recorded music. Alternatively, you could sing 'Worthy is the Lamb' very quietly several times.

▶ The healing ministry of Jesus (Part 2)

The balance between proclamation and demonstration

Jesus frequently used situations where someone was healed as stepping-stones to teach important truths. There are several examples of this combination, such as Luke 13:10–17, the woman whom Satan had bound; John 9, the man born blind; and Mark 2:1–12, the paralysed man. We see the same pattern in the earliest days of the church after Pentecost, when Peter used the healing of the lame man as a natural way in to preaching about Jesus (Acts 3).

The ministry of Jesus was one of proclamation and demonstration. (See OHP 7.)

Group Bible study

→ Divide the group into pairs or small sub-groups and allocate the account of a healing to each group. Ask them to discover what essential truth Jesus was teaching through the healing event. Share your results.

Possible accounts:

Mark 2:1–12	The healing of the paralytic
Mark 3:1–6	The man with the shrivelled hand
Mark 9:14–29	The boy with an evil spirit
Luke 13:10–17	The crippled woman
Luke 19:1–10	The 'healing' of Zacchaeus
John 9:1–41	The man born blind
Acts 3	The crippled beggar healed by Peter and John

Group discussion (optional)

→ Luke tells us that Jesus sent his disciples out to 'preach the kingdom of God and to heal the sick' (Luke 9:2). What practical steps should your church be taking to ensure a balance between proclamation and action in the ministry of healing?

The balance between love and power

These elements often get out of balance in our ministry but were held in perfect balance in the ministry of Jesus. Take for example the raising of Jairus's daughter. There is an incredible display of divine power in raising her from the dead, and this is immediately followed by the down-to-earth, compassionate command, 'Give her something to eat' (Luke 8:41–56; Mark 5:21–43). It is worth noting, too, that the raising of Jairus's daughter follows the healing of the woman in the crowd, where Jesus makes the observation that power has gone from him (Luke 8:46).

In the church's ministry of healing, both love and power should be demonstrated. We need as much power for healing as possible, but this must be exercised with as much love as possible. What tends to happen in practice is that a church will become out of balance in its approach. Where love and power are both maximised we will see them demonstrated in a number of ways. (See OHP 8.)

Love (pastoral emphasis)
● Emphasis on the person seeking healing.
● Emphasis on pastoral care and counselling.
● Often the ministry will be spread over a long period of time and broadened to include all sorts of areas in the person's life.
● Practical help.

Power (evangelistic emphasis)
● Emphasis on God and his promises.
● Emphasis on proclamation (gift of knowledge, etc).
● Emphasis on prayer to God rather than counselling of the person.
● Use of prayers of command for healing, release or deliverance. Looking for evidence of the Holy Spirit's power, eg shaking, weeping, etc.

Obviously these two lists do not accurately reflect every situation. (Session 8 will look in more detail at signs of God's power being released in the Christian community.)

Group activity
➔ Invite a general discussion about the two emphases. Do individuals have any personal preference, and if so do they know why? The aim is to show that both are vital and complement one another.

Another way of looking at this is to consider the character of Jesus. There are those who say they want to be 'like Jesus', meaning that they would like their personality to be in line with his character, but who at the same time shun the gifting of the Holy Spirit. There may be several reasons for this:

● The expression of the character of Christ may be more culturally acceptable than gifts of the Holy Spirit.
● The use of gifts of the Spirit may move us to a place where our faith is tested.
● There may be a fear of the supernatural – 'Is this really of God?'

Power and authority (optional section)

When Jesus sent the disciples out to 'preach the kingdom of God and to heal the sick', he gave them the necessary equipment for the task (Luke 9:1–2). Jesus, who is the 'same yesterday and today and for ever' (Hebrews 13:8), does the same for us. That equipment can be summed up in the two words 'power' and 'authority'. Both qualities are demonstrated in the ministry of Jesus. He obviously has power to heal all types of sickness, to cast out demons and to raise the dead, but it was equally clear that he acted with the authority of God (John 5:16–30).

Giving his disciples the power to heal is not enough. (Some occultists have power to heal.) Giving his disciples the authority to heal is not enough, for they still need the power. Both are required. (There will be times when it will be appropriate to use a 'command' prayer; for example, 'In Jesus' name receive your healing.')

We can only know the authority of Jesus in our prayers if we ourselves are firmly under his authority (Matthew 8:5–13).

Optional group activity
→ Draw out the distinction between power and authority in modern situations. For example, a policeman has the authority to stop a lorry, but only the lorry driver has the power through the brake pedal to stop the vehicle. Think of other examples.

The healing ministry of Jesus and the kingdom of God

Jesus saw healing as a sign of the kingdom of God coming among men, women and children. This kingdom was not a military or political one, of the sort longed for by the people of Israel, but rather the kingdom that 'is within you' (Luke 17:21). The kingdom of God is not a political state; it is rather a spiritual state. It is where the rule of God is established, and where there is harmony and wholeness.

This is why Jesus instructed his disciples to 'preach the kingdom and heal the sick' (Luke 9:2). Proclamation of this kingdom will inevitably bring us into conflict with Satan. The healing ministry to which we are called opposes Satan, who is described as the 'thief who comes only to steal and kill and destroy', for it will proclaim Jesus, who says, 'I have come that they may have life, and have it to the full' (John 10:10). (What a wonderful contrast is contained in that one verse of Scripture!) Jesus also made it clear that his sacrificial death upon the cross would herald the ultimate downfall of Satan.

> 'Now is the time for judgment on this world; now the prince of this world will be driven out. But I, when I am lifted up from the earth, will draw all men to myself.'
>
> (John 12:31–32)

● Jesus preached the kingdom of God (Mark 1:14–15; Matthew 4:23 and 9:35).

- The disciples were told by Jesus to preach it (Luke 9:1–2; Matthew 10:1–8).
- The 72 others were told to preach it (Luke 10:1–9).

The Old Testament view of a military state, like the Davidic kingdom, waned as time went by and was superseded by the idea of the 'Day of the Lord'. The prophets expected God to intervene in history, but this in turn gave place to the idea that the coming of the kingdom would usher in the end of history. It would be the time of the final downfall of Satan (Daniel 2:44). Jesus was born into this culture, and the writers of the New Testament saw Jesus (particularly in his death and resurrection) as a sign of God's kingdom. Although Jesus brought in this new age, however, it is still not here in its completeness. The decisive battle is won but we are still engaged in the mopping-up operations.

▶ Beginning to look at our own ministry

Hopes and fears

As we begin to move into our own participation in the healing ministry of Christ, various questions will begin to surface from the group members. Allow time for people to discuss their hopes and fears, and at an appropriate point introduce the questionnaire.

The questionnaire

The questionnaire is an important step in the learning process of this course. In introducing the questionnaire you need to stress that it is not an examination. (The questionnaire is printed in the linkwork book as Appendix A.)

The questionnaire is a tool to help the leader and the group members to discover just where they are in their thinking and experience of the Christian ministry of healing. Use it in the way you feel will most help the members of your group. Will you go through the answers individually with each member? In this case you need to make appointments to see each person. (This is the ideal but it is very costly in terms of time and commitment.)

Stress that the questionnaire is there to help group members take stock at the halfway point in the course.

▶ Ways of praying for healing (5)

Using the gift of tongues

Introduce tongues as one 'tool' in the prayer kit! A very matter-of-fact approach at this stage may help people to see this as a natural part of the Christian experience. Allow time for questions and expressions of any anxiety. Stress the usefulness of the gift of tongues in prayer, particularly when you do not know exactly how to pray in a particular situation.

Explain how praying in tongues can act as a catalyst, enabling other gifts of the Holy Spirit to operate, particularly the gift of knowledge. Allow time for group members to ask their own questions about this prayer gift, and possibly to tell their own stories about its use.

> 'In the same way, the Spirit helps us in our weakness. We do not know what we ought to pray, but the Spirit himself intercedes for us with groans that words cannot express.'
>
> (Romans 8:26)

How can I pray in tongues?

God loves to give (Luke 15:22) and God loves you (John 3:16). All gifts are an outworking of God's love. God has already given his Son Jesus on the cross for you. Having done this surely there is no reason why he should withhold spiritual gifts! Be open to God (Revelation 3:20). Remember – ask and it will be given to you (Luke 11:9). Praise God in your own language and then, having asked for the gift, dare to speak in words you do not know, trusting in his presence and power. Ask a friend or group of friends who use this gift to pray with you. Encourage this gift but do not strive or become intense. If prayer in tongues does not take place at this time, go on seeking in the days to come.

Some additional notes on prayer in tongues

Prayer in tongues uses a language not understood by the user but under the user's control (1 Corinthians 14:32). It is therefore not ecstatic. It will not harm us (Luke 11:11–13). It has the sound of real language and beauty. Prayer in tongues has great value.

- In our relationship with God, prayer in tongues enables us to speak directly to him from the depths of our being, in praise (1 Corinthians 14:2 and 14:15; Acts 10:44–46). It helps the speaker because it is an outward, visible sign of surrender to God. It stills our mind (1 Corinthians 14:14) and enables God to give other gifts, like supernatural knowledge.
- In prayer meetings the gift of tongues can help the church listen to God. The church must also test the gifts of the Holy Spirit (1 Corinthians 14:13). Tongues must be used sparingly, with order, and above all in love (1 Corinthians 13 and 14). Praying in tongues can move the church into expecting supernatural signs.
- As a sign to unbelievers, speaking in tongues will provoke questions and open the way to witnessing (1 Peter 3:15). An atmosphere of worship can have a converting effect (Acts 2).

Tongues was the first spiritual gift used after Pentecost (Acts 2:4). It must not be seen as a mark of superiority or a necessary sign of being filled with the Holy Spirit; this is unscriptural and divisive. In 1 Corinthians 14:5 it is implied that not all had this gift in New Testament times, but Paul encouraged all to seek it.

▸ Worship, prayer and ministry

It may be right to invite the Holy Spirit to come with his loving power on the group. Obviously you will only do this if you feel it is right and if you are fairly sure that the group is ready. Should you decide to proceed, the following order of worship may be of help.

- Explanation. We have talked about how Jesus combined divine power and love. We can experience this power and love for ourselves and for others by asking the Holy Spirit of God to come into our lives. When he comes he fills us with God's love, for 'God has poured out his love into our hearts by the Holy Spirit, whom he has given us' (Romans 5:5). He also comes with divine power: '. . . but stay in the city until you have been clothed with power from on high' (Luke 24:49). Keep the explanation as brief as possible, and then invite the Holy Spirit to come, either by singing a song or hymn which invokes the Holy Spirit, or by a simple prayer.
- Stillness. Quietly watch for signs of the Holy Spirit's anointing and thank God for it. (Session 5 of *Life in the Spirit* may provide useful background reading for this part of the ministry.)
- Prayer. Pray for each person on the intercession list: 'Holy Spirit of God, come to John as he recovers.' 'Holy Spirit of God, come to Mary.'
- Bible reading (Ephesians 3:14–21).
- A hymn or song of praise (for example 'O for a thousand tongues').

Preparation for the next session

If you are using group members to lead the worship, tell them now what you would like them to do during the prayer time at the next session.

If you are going to see each person between sessions to talk through their response to the questionnaire, make sure the appointments are made, and ask people to make time to think through the questionnaire before the appointment.

You should draw the attention of the group members to the prayer for the filling with the Holy Spirit which is set out in the link-work books (Appendix C) if you intend to use this prayer in the next session. If you are using some different form then it will be helpful to explain to group members what you hope to do in the next session, so that they have time to prepare.

■ Resources for Session 5

- OHP diagrams for this session
    - OHP 7, Balance in the healing ministry of Jesus
    - OHP 8, Balance between evangelical and pastoral approaches to healing
- The balance between love and power source material:
    - Michael Green, *I Believe in the Holy Spirit*, Hodder 1985. See particularly chapters 9 and 10, 'The Spirit's fullness' and 'The Spirit's gifts'.
    - Tom Wright, *A Moment of Prayer*, Lion Publishing 1997. Tom describes prayer in tongues in several ways (eg 'Praying in tongues . . . is the flutter of a flag in the breeze, showing that the King is in residence'). It is helpful to show how a scholar like Tom Wright can write naturally and effectively about this gift.
    - Arthur Wallis, *Pray in the Spirit*, Kingsway 1970.
    - *A Time to Heal – The Development of Good Practice in the Healing Ministry – A Handbook*, Church House Publishing 2000. This booklet could well be given to all group members at this point.

6 Equipped for ministry

 ## Aims

- To give course members confidence to step out in faith in Christian healing.
- To introduce, or review, what it means to be filled with the Holy Spirit.

 ## Outline and timing

0–10 mins   Getting started
- Short review of course so far
- Opening prayer

10–40   Main learning focus: How the Holy Spirit equips us for ministry
- Channels of his grace
- Filled with the Holy Spirit
- The gifts of the Holy Spirit
- 'Rivers of living water'
- Clean vessels

40–70   Ministry: 'Open to the Holy Spirit'

70–85   Ways of praying for healing (6)
- Intercessory prayer

85–90   Closing prayer

 ## Running Session 6

By now the group should have an overview of some aspects of praying together – both for one another and for people whom they know who are in need of their prayers. They may already have seen answers to their prayers, and this will encourage everyone.

The teaching content of this session is deliberately shortened to give plenty of time to minister to group members. Keep the introduction very brief, and push on through the teaching section. Concentrate especially on praying for all members to be filled with the Holy Spirit. Pray before the session that the Lord will minister to his people.

Get the emphasis right!

The vital emphasis must be upon God the Holy Trinity, who wants to heal and to give us the grace and power to be agents of his healing.

> 'Remain in me and I will remain in you. No branch can bear fruit by itself: It must remain in the vine.'
>
> (John 15:4)
>
> 'In the same way, the Spirit helps us in our weakness. We do not know what we ought to pray, but the Spirit himself intercedes for us with groans that words cannot express.'
>
> (Romans 8:26)

To bring the healing love of Christ to others we need to have his love 'poured out . . . into our hearts by the Holy Spirit, whom he has given us' (Romans 5:5), and we must be under his authority.

At this stage in the course we are challenging people with the need to be 'clothed with power from on high'. Some who are taking part in this course may have worked through the *Life in the Spirit* course and come to the point where they have already asked God to baptise them in the power of the Holy Spirit. There may be others on the course who have not taken that step and they should be encouraged to do so. Every member of the course should face the fact that to bring the healing power of God to others we must be channels of his grace and open to everything he wants to give us.

You will need to outline the basic theology of what it means to be 'clothed with power' or 'baptised in the Holy Spirit'. Even if every-one in your group has been through similar material before, this recap is still important. Allow plenty of time for discussion, but avoid the trap of spending the whole evening talking and not leaving plenty of time for prayer and ministry.

Preparation

- Pray for all those you expect to come, asking the Lord to protect them as they come to the meeting.
- Have large sheets of paper and coloured markers ready for group work and for other notes or lists.
- Prepare three glasses:
  - A clean glass filled with clean water.
  - A dirty glass filled with clean water.
  - A clean glass filled with dirty water.

Opening prayer

Concentrate on thanksgiving for what God has done in the group. Share how the people you are praying for are getting on, and give thanks for what God has done in their lives.

Note that the main time of prayer and ministry is put in the middle of this evening. This is to allow plenty of time to pray for people to be filled with the Holy Spirit.

▶ Filled with the Holy Spirit

Five key biblical instructions

For the power of the Holy Spirit to fill us, we need to do five things. Outline these five points very briefly. The discussion that follows will show you where you need to add further explanation. (See OHP 9.)

1. *Thirst*. We must want this power and yearn for it, not for ourselves but for the common good. This yearning is the work of the Spirit and is referred to as 'thirsting' in John 7:37ff. (Note how the waters of life flow out of the person.) Hopefully the course will have brought people to this point.
2. *Repent*. Our old way of life must be subject to a radical turn round, with Jesus as Lord. Repentance will include confession

of any unconfessed sin, and the renunciation of evil, but it will go much further than this (Acts 2:38).

3. *Ask* to be filled with the Holy Spirit. God wants to fill us with himself. In asking to be filled with the Holy Spirit we declare that we are willing for this to happen (Luke 11:1–13).

4. *Believe* the promises of God. We may not feel any different, and we may have to wait for a while, as the disciples did (Luke 24:49). Assure group members that if they ask sincerely then God will fill them with his Holy Spirit (Luke 11:10–13). You may also need to remind people that the Holy Spirit will not hurt us when he comes in power into our lives.

5. *Obey.* 'The Holy Spirit, whom God has given to those who obey him' (Acts 5:32). It is not uncommon for people to become convinced that God has filled them with his Holy Spirit when they step out in faith and obey an inner nudge of the Holy Spirit, often with dramatic results.

The use of personal testimony from group members will be invaluable as you work your way through this section. Refer to the prayer of commitment set out in Appendix C of the link-work books.

Spiritual gifts in healing (see 1 Corinthians 12–14)

● Word of knowledge. When the Holy Spirit wishes to inform us of a particular truth at a particular time about person or situation, he can give a picture, a word, a pain (indicating where the person being prayed with is in pain), etc. If we receive such a 'knowledge' about another person we must use such information with great sensitivity (cf. Jesus and the woman at the well in John 4:1–26).

● Word of wisdom. This is an utterance inspired by God, which will often short cut a prolonged discussion or argument.

● Prophecy. This is when God speaks through an individual to encourage or warn. Often this gift is important when a church is seeking God's will about what sort of healing ministry should be set up. (See Session 9.)

● Prayer in tongues and the interpretation of tongues. This gift was examined in some detail during Session 5. If it is used during a time of ministry it can act as a catalyst for other gifts, particularly knowledge. When a ministry team is open to the Holy Spirit it is often possible to experience groupings of gifts, each one helping towards our understanding of how we should pray in the particular situation.

● Gift of faith. (See Session 4.) This is a deep and overwhelming conviction that God will act in a specific way in a particular situation. It is a transrational certainty and assurance that God is about to act.

● Gifts of healings. Note that this is in the plural, probably indicating that just as there are many different medical and surgical techniques, there is also a variety of ways in which the Lord heals.

● Miracles. These are events which are visibly obvious to those who see them, often when we are radically obedient to God. Some would argue that the word 'miracle' should only be used in connection with inanimate things (eg the multiplication of food) and should not be used of healing. The word 'miracle' is often used when something happens suddenly. Thus if a cut hand instantly heals during prayer we might speak of a miracle. Yet is the process perhaps the same as the normal healing of a cut hand, but speeded up?

● Discernment of spirits. Many people involved in the Christian ministry of healing sense when they are dealing with a malign spiritual force. (See Session 8.)

Group discussion
➔ Invite people to share their own experiences. Many will have experienced gifts of knowledge but maybe not understood what they were. For example, 'knowing' that a friend was in trouble and phoning them just at the right moment.

Bible study on 'rivers of living water'
Take the whole group quickly through the following Bible references and then move on to the visual aid with the glasses, called 'Channels of his grace'. In some New Age circles channelling carries the idea of spiritualist mediumship. You should make it quite clear that this is not what we mean by channelling!

● Ezekiel 47:1–12. Water flows from the temple. It brings life and vitality. Plants grow along its banks. The fruit serve for food and the leaves for healing.

- Revelation 22:1–5. The theme is repeated, but this time the water flows from the throne of God and of the Lamb. Again it brings healing and also removes the curse.
- Revelation 22:17: 'The Spirit and the bride say, "Come!" And let him who hears say, "Come!" Whoever is thirsty, let him come; and whoever wishes, let him take the free gift of the water of life.' The bride symbolises the church. The church, together with the Holy Spirit, invites us to come and to drink of this living water.
- John 7:37. Note the three states of thirsting, coming and drinking. Jesus declares that streams of living water will flow from within those who believe in him.

Group activity – channels of his grace

→ This simple visual aid can be very helpful and it follows on from the Bible study. Produce the three glasses which have been prepared in advance (see introductory notes to this session).
  - Glass 1 will be perfectly clean and full of clean water.
  - Glass 2 will have had brown shoe polish smeared round it (it looks revolting), and will then be filled with clean water.
  - Glass 3 will be clean but will be filled with dirty water.

Ask the group to discuss the meaning of the symbolism of the three glasses. The water represents the healing grace of God. The glasses represent people who are channels of this grace. Ideally we need pure water from a clean glass. The dirty glass represents people who have allowed sin to continue in their life. The power of the Holy Spirit can flow through them, but they are not allowing him to flow in them, to convict them of sin and lead them to repentance. The dirty water represents the healing grace of God which has been contaminated by psychic and satanic elements. It must be made clear that those involved in the Christian healing ministry should never be involved in such practices.

We are channels through the power of the Holy Spirit of the healing grace of God the creator through the mediation of his only begotten Son, Jesus Christ.

▶ Ministry – 'Open to the Spirit'

Do not allow this time of prayer to be eroded by too much teaching or discussion. Remember that this time of ministry is the most important part of the evening, and as such is set in the middle of the evening rather than left to the end. A simple form of prayer, asking God to fill a person with his Holy Spirit, is contained in Appendix D of this manual and also in the link-work books in Appendix C.

Pray for guidance about how you should conduct this ministry. Tell the group what you intend to do in simple direct terms – then get on with it! There is always pressure to delay this prayer, but resist it (1 Peter 5:9).

▶ Ways of praying for healing (6)

Intercessory prayer

'We are called, near to Jesus and with Jesus and in Jesus to be with God with the people in our heart . . . you with God for the people, and you with the people in God's strength.'
(Michael Ramsey, *The Christian Priest Today*, SPCK 1974)

There are many questions which people love to discuss about intercessory prayer. Should we have lists of people? Should we keep a diary, marking dates when we see answers to prayer? Allow the discussion to range freely and draw out from people what their particular practice is. Different styles suit different people. There is no right or wrong way, but it is important to emphasise that we should be prepared to experiment and discover new methods.

Those who find lists difficult may find the following method helpful. Write the names of those you wish to pray for on separate pieces of paper, and place them in a box or envelope. Have another box or envelope ready, and during your prayer time take two or three at random from the first container, pray for them and then transfer them into the other receptacle. During your next prayer time do the same, and so on. When you have prayed for them all, reverse the process!

Praying in the name of Jesus

This is not a magic formula. You could help people understand this by having a blank cheque, written but not signed. As soon as you sign it, the paper has the power to transfer money (provided you have it in your account in the first place!). The resources of Jesus are limitless and 'with God nothing is impossible'.

Another example is a petition. Would Jesus sign it? In other words, is your prayer in agreement with his will? Praying in the name of Jesus carries with it both a great blessing but also a great responsibility – to pray according to his will.

A pattern for intercession

- A time of adoration, using hymns and spiritual songs of praise, psalms, canticles, etc.
- A time of total stillness, looking at Jesus, perhaps contemplating some of his words, or using faith imagination to picture a healing miracle.
- Lovingly remembering people for whom we are praying. Again we may well use our imaginations to enter into their suffering.
- A time of thanksgiving.

Prayer

If you have not spent time earlier in the evening, pray now for people to be filled with the Holy Spirit, then use the above pattern in your prayer time. Major on listening to God.

Preparation for next session

You will probably already have dealt with some of the hard questions that inevitably come up when thinking about the healing ministry. You could ask your group to jot down questions that puzzle them or concern them, ready for next week's session entitled 'God and the mystery of suffering'.

Resources for Session 6

- OHP diagram for this session
  - OHP 9, Filled with the Holy Spirit – five key biblical instructions
- Equipped for ministry source material
  - Read through the notes for Sessions 5–7 of the *Saints Alive! Life in the Spirit* Leaders Manual, particularly Session 5. See also Appendix D of this manual for a form of prayer which is also printed out in the link-work book.
  - Roy Lawrence, *The Practice of Christian Healing*, Triangle 1998.

7 God and the mystery of suffering

 ## Aim

- To examine some of the difficult questions about suffering, death and the mystery of 'unanswered' prayer.

 ## Outline and timing

0–30 mins   Getting started
- Opening worship
- Review of progress so far, particularly in the light of last week's ministry
- Dealing with questions about gifts of the Holy Spirit

30–55   Main learning focus: The healing ministry, suffering and death
- Suffering
- Growing old and dying
- Chronic illness

Possible refreshment break

55–70   Main learning focus (continued)
- How do we face the mystery of unanswered prayer?

70–80   Ways of praying for healing (7)
- Praying when people are not healed
- Persistence in prayer and 'soaking prayer'

80–90   Worship and prayer

 Running Session 7

The whole of the session is envisaged as a general group discussion.

A careful reading of *A Time to Heal*, chapter 12, 'Questions people ask about the healing ministry', would be time well spent before you lead this session.

By now the group should be well established and everyone should be able to contribute. Each section is followed by a group discussion period. It is suggested that the leader speaks briefly about the material in the book and then opens up the discussion. There are two fundamental areas around which most questions will centre:

1.   Why does an all-loving, all-powerful God allow suffering?
2.   Why does healing, after prayer, not always happen?

This is not an easy subject. Do not worry if the discussion becomes wide-ranging, as long as you cover the main issues during the evening. OHP 10. 'The mystery of suffering', could be shown at different times during the session.

Preparation

The leader should prepare carefully, thinking through the questions raised in the teaching session. There are several books recommended in the book list for this session, and dipping into some of these may also be a good method of preparation. In leading this session the leader should:

● Be aware that this subject touches everyone deeply. There are no complete answers so we find ourselves entering into a mystery.
● Avoid becoming negative. Keep your eyes on Jesus, not on the problems.
● Beware of dualism. Put crudely, this is the belief that all suffering is from the devil and that there is a struggle between God and the devil – who are more or less equally matched – but our prayer

and ministry shift the balance in God's favour. When stated like this the danger of dualism is highlighted. A child in a Southern Baptist Sunday school put it this way: 'God created the bee, the devil created the stinger!'

- Highlight the need to avoid putting guilt on people by suggesting they need more faith or obedience.
- Discourage pious statements that avoid facing the real problem (eg 'God's good, isn't he?').
- Take care not to spend too long with the personal experiences or problems of any one group member.

▶ The mystery of suffering

Jesus reveals the nature of the Father

- 'Anyone who has seen me has seen the Father' (John 14:9).
- 'For in Christ all the fulness of the Deity lives in bodily form' (Colossians 2:9).

Jesus fought against sickness and disease. As he uniquely reveals God the Father to us then we have to face further questions.

Group activity
→ What sort of God does Jesus reveal? Quickly make a list of the sort of adjectives that might be used to describe God.

How can a good God allow suffering?

The mystery of suffering exists because we believe in the God as revealed to us by Jesus. If there is no God then suffering is just a matter of chance.

One possible solution to the problem is to say that God does not involve himself in the affairs of the world any more. It's a sort of divine experiment which has been set up and is now left to run and God does not intervene. If this hypothesis is true, then any attempt to pray for healing would be futile. However, the God revealed to us in Scripture is incarnational: 'The word became flesh and dwelt among us.' God is changeless. He would not show intense concern for the world and its suffering by sending Jesus at one time in history and then ignore the world subsequently!

A second possible solution is to say that God is good and he does care, but suffering is the direct or indirect result of the Fall. Suffering is the work of evil forces (Satan is the prince of this world), and our praying and ministry against suffering is part of the battle to re-establish the kingdom of God on earth: 'Thy kingdom come on earth as in Heaven.' This solution is more in line with the teaching of God's word, but it still leaves us with some unanswered questions. If God is all-powerful and Jesus won the ultimate victory over Satan on the cross, why is suffering still allowed to continue? There is a danger here of falling into dualism, seeing the forces of chaos and the forces for wholeness matched in some combat of equals.

A third argument is that the process of creating order out of chaos (Genesis 1) is still going on. The earthquakes, floods, congenital deformities and disease, the appearance of new, mutated viruses, etc, are all part of a process in which the 'whole creation has been groaning as in the pains of childbirth right up to the present time' (Romans 8:22). This view allows for the problems we have with chaos, and it sees our ministry as a co-operation with God in an ongoing process towards ultimate wholeness.

'God's kingdom is creation healed.'
(Hans Kung, *On Being a Christian*, Collins 1977)

Group activity
➔ Discuss the three alternatives summarised above. In what ways are they helpful, and in what ways are they unhelpful?

A mystery rather than a problem

If we think in terms of the mystery of suffering rather than the problem of suffering we may be helped. We enter into a mystery and in a sense become part of it. The mystery of suffering is not a problem that can be solved; there are no totally satisfactory answers available to us in this life. It is acceptable to admit that we do not understand, provided we have struggled as far as we can with the problem. Our wrestling in prayer will mean that we enter more deeply into the mystery of suffering. Only Jesus Christ entered fully into this mystery in all its horror on the cross.

Group discussion

➔ Divide the group into pairs to discuss the question: 'Is there any occasion in your life when you felt that you had entered into the mystery of suffering? What did you learn from your experience?'

God's will and natural law

If you cut your finger, your body immediately starts processes which lead to the healing of the cut. Some will argue that this indicates it is God's nature to heal. Others take a different line. It is natural, they say, for all living things to reproduce and then die. Death of individuals but survival of the species is the natural law. For the Christian this raises the question, 'Is death a part of God's plan, or is death in fact the last enemy?'

Group discussion

➔ In what ways do you regard death as 'the last enemy to be destroyed' and in what ways do you see death as a gateway into the nearer presence of God? Is there such a thing as 'untimely death' and if so how would you define it?

The place of death

If we see death as the absolute end of our personal existence, then healing will be seen in terms of putting off death for as long as possible. The Christian view is that true healing involves a relationship with Jesus who is 'the resurrection and the life'. This raises ethical problems for those involved in medicine. It also raises problems of how we pray for those whose lives are nearly over. Everyone Jesus healed died eventually. When we pray for healing are we prepared, if we feel it is in God's will, to pray for a peaceful death? (See Session 4, 'Faith when things get tough'.)

Is pain a good thing?

Pain is a warning signal and often the first step to healing. But what about meaningless, chronic, grinding pain, which no longer serves a purpose in telling us something is wrong? Do we see the plants and chemicals from which drugs can be derived to relieve pain as the gift of a good God for us?

Can suffering be redemptive?

There has been a long tradition among Christians that pain can be offered to God and, through some mystery, contribute to the process of healing in individuals and society. Some may be called to this hidden ministry, but a glib statement like 'It's a cross I have to bear' is often used to escape from the real tension of wrestling in prayer about disease. The most authentic accounts of redemptive suffering are from people who have spent years praying for healing and only reluctantly, and very gradually, discovered this unique vocation.

Why does God heal some people and not others?

Here we face head on the mystery of unanswered prayer. Francis MacNutt in his book *Healing* lists eleven reasons why people are not healed when prayer is offered. He writes, 'The best point of view, I think, is to see that God's normative will is that people will be healed, unless there is some countervailing reason.' The following summary is useful, although baldly stated like this the reasons appear negative, and one needs to read the relevant chapter in Francis MacNutt's book. I would personally wish to place 'lack of faith' lower down the list, because it produces false guilt in so many people.

See OHP 11. (List based on section headings in chapter entitled 'Eleven reasons why people are not healed' in *Healing* by Francis MacNutt, Hodder 1997.)

1. Lack of faith
2. A false value placed on suffering
3. Sick person called to redemptive suffering
4. Sin in patient or minister blocking prayer
5. Not praying specifically
6. Not praying into the real cause of the sickness

7. Refusal to see God's healing in medicine
8. Not taking care of our body
9. Now is not the time
10. A different person called to pray
11. Environment prevents healing

The mystery of the nature of God

'It's God they ought to crucify instead of you and me
I said to the carpenter a-hanging on the tree.'

(Sidney Carter)

Job cries out at one point, 'He (God) is not a man like me that I might answer him, that we might confront each other in court. If only there were someone to arbitrate between us, to lay his hand upon us both, someone to remove God's rod from me, so that his terror would frighten me no more. Then I would speak up without fear of him, but as it now stands with me, I cannot' (Job 9:32–35). The Christian answer is that there is someone – it is our Lord and Saviour, Jesus Christ.

Group Bible meditation
→ Read Isaiah 53 slowly and carefully aloud to the group. First pray that the Holy Spirit will open ears, minds and hearts. Perhaps consider reading the passage against very quiet background music.

Keep silence, then invite open prayer of adoration.

Growing old and dying
(Background reading – *A Time to Heal*, chapter 8, page 153 ff.)

Teilard de Chardin, in *Le Milieu Divin* (Fontana 1957), speaks of two phases in our lives. Each can be divinised – that is, given to God for him to transform. He speaks of the divinisation of activities and the divinisation of passivities. The divinisation of our passivities he defines as 'that which is not done by us'.

Ageing and dying happen to us. They force us to 'live with loss'. The passivities that affect us have to be 'lived with'. Doctors often encourage their patients to 'live with' a condition. Thus we speak today of people living with cancer, rather than dying from cancer. Much of a general practitioner's work will be in providing drugs, therapies and encouragement to patients to help them make the best of life in spite of chronic pain, disability or sickness.

Chronic illness – how should we pray?

A member of the church comes for prayer. Her doctor has told her that although he can prescribe painkilling drugs for her arthritic condition, there is little else that he can do. She has always been active, and dislikes the thought of having to rely on tablets. She is a person of great faith, believing that God healed her daughter from cancer at the age of 40. She believes God can heal her and remove her pain at this moment.

What would you say to her? How would you pray for her?

This case history brings several issues into focus. Everyone comes to prayer for healing with expectations. These may not be expressed, or even consciously acknowledged. For example:

- A person may be positive that God will heal, but frankly unrealistic in their expectations. (But see the next scenario.)
- They may be positive that God will heal and, although this is unlikely medically, the person has been given a gift of faith that wonderful healing will take place in this case. (Note the subtle difference to the first scenario.)
- They may feel negative, not expecting much to happen, but 'will try anything once'.
- A person may be uncertain about what will happen, but comes with 'an open mind'.
- They may be uncertain about what will happen, but come in the sure knowledge that they are putting the matter in God's hands.

At the same time, those who minister also have expectations. For example:

- 'We have prayed for this person so many times. Nothing will happen.' (Negative.)
- 'If this person were healed what a witness that would be!' (Wrong motive.)
- A gift of faith. (Positive.)
- 'I am convinced of the love of God for this person. I am prepared to risk entering into the mystery of prayer for the sick.' (Positive.)

Group discussion

→ Now let's go back to the illustration of the lady with arthritis. Ask the group the following questions:

- What do you think her expectations will be?
- Imagine that her expectation is that God will instantly heal her. How will you react and pray?
- Imagine she admits to you that she has little faith that God can heal, though she has pretended to have a lot of faith. How will you proceed?

Some pointers when praying for those who are chronically sick:

- Try to understand how they feel about the prospect of ongoing suffering.
- Encourage honesty in facing the situation. It is not a lack of faith to face suffering realistically.
- Try to deepen the person's trust in a loving God who cares about their situation as it is now.
- If the person is housebound, arrange for someone to visit and pray with them regularly.
- Give the person an ongoing task (like Bible readings).
- Encourage them to become prayer warriors for the ministry of your church. (One effect of chronic illness is the feeling that one is becoming increasingly useless, but people who suffer chronic conditions are often mighty prayer warriors.)
- In prayer, bring the person into close contact with Jesus.
- Pray for an anointing of the Holy Spirit upon them.
- Encourage thankfulness.
- Show love and consideration.

- Use short, well-known and meaningful prayers and words of Scripture to 'feed' them.
- Expect to see signs of God's love worked out in their lives, and help them to see these too.

▶ Ways of praying for healing (7)

Deal with any wrong attitudes in yourself which may hinder your prayers. If prayer is not answered, the first question to be asked is, 'Lord, is there something that needs healing in me?' This may be a bad relationship or a root of bitterness which needs to be confessed. (See Matthew 5:23–24.) At the same time, do not be burdened with guilt. Remember the Lord puts us right; he never puts us down.

Praying when people are not healed

- Avoid the kind of prayer which is designed to help us ignore the pain.
- In your mind, go through the check list of why people are not healed and ask if any of these factors apply to the situation. If anything comes into focus, gently minister to that point.
- Be thankful! It is easy to get bogged down in a difficult situation, so remember some of the times when you have seen the healing grace of God in action.
- Do not strive. Ask the Holy Spirit to guide you about how you should pray and simply obey any idea that you may have. Learn to 'let go and let God'.
- Having done as much as you can, do not fret or become intense about the problem. Trust the sick person to God's love.
- Sometimes the Holy Spirit speaks to us as we stop struggling.
- Don't become obsessed about your apparent 'failure'.
- Don't let this problem stop you going on in faith in the Christian ministry of healing.

Persistence in prayer and 'soaking prayer'

When things get difficult we need to persist in prayer, bearing in mind the cautions listed above – particularly about not striving.

Jesus teaches in Luke 18:1–8 the lessons of persistence. 'Be alert and always keep on praying,' is Paul's instruction to the Ephesians (6:18). The difference between persistence in prayer and 'striving' is that the former is enabled by the Holy Spirit, while the latter is done by human effort and is exhausting.

This persistence may be necessary for several reasons:

- As a demonstration of our own love and concern for the person we are praying for.
- As a demonstration of our own love and trust in God to whom we are praying, even though at first there seems to be no answer.
- As a challenge to any dark forces which may be blocking our prayers (see Daniel 10:13).

Soaking prayer may take the form of praying for a person every day. Members of a church healing team could perhaps teach members of the family to lay hands with prayer on the sick family member every day over a period of time.

▶ Worship and prayer

It may be helpful to read one or two accounts of dramatic healings which have taken place in the context of Christian prayer. Focus the prayer time on thanksgiving and praise. Concentrate on God and his goodness. One suggested hymn could be 'God is working his purpose out'.

Preparation for next session

The next session's focus is on helping those involved in the occult. The group should be encouraged to pray for protection for each other during the coming week, but try not to raise alarm about this. If you are delegating the worship to group members, tell them to focus upon the presence of the Holy Spirit and asking the angels of God to guard and protect the meeting next week. For the Bible reading, a passage like Ephesians 6:10–18 or 2 Corinthians 10:4–5 would provide encouragement.

Resources for Session 7

- OHP diagrams for this session
  - OHP 10. This can be used at intervals during the whole session. It is designed to portray the idea of entering into the mystery of suffering, with the cross at the centre of the questions.
  - OHP 11, Why some are not healed. Read *Healing* by Francis MacNutt, especially chapter 18, 'Eleven reasons why people are not healed', as a background to the OHP summary.
- The mystery of suffering source material:
  - C. S. Lewis, *The Problem of Pain*, Fount 1998.
  - C. S. Lewis, *A Grief Observed*, Faber 1966.
  - David Watson, *Fear no Evil*, Hodder and Stoughton 1998.
  - John Richards (ed), *The Church's Healing Ministry*, Marshall Pickering 1986. This is an abridged summary of the Report of the Archbishops' Commission into the church's ministry of healing.
  - *A Time to Heal* report, chapter 12, pages 222 ff.
  - Roy Lawrence, *How to Pray When Life Hurts*, Scripture Union 1993.

8 Our ministry in practice

 Aims

- To encourage good practice in the church's healing ministry.
- To prepare course members for difficult situations that may arise in this ministry.

Outline and timing

0–10 mins	Getting started
	• Short review
	• Opening worship
10–40	Main learning focus: Ministry in practice
	• Guidelines for good practice in the church's healing ministry
	• Praying with children
	• Laying on of hands with prayer
40–55	Areas which can cause concern
	• Helping people who have been involved in alternative medicine, or occult practices
55–70	Moving on in ministry
	• Outward, visible signs of the Holy Spirit's activity
	• Bible study on the words Jesus used when praying for the sick
70–80	Ways of praying for healing (8)
	• The prayer of command
80–90	Worship and prayer

Running Session 8

This session, dealing as it does with practical matters, presents particular challenges to the leader. First, there is the challenge to remain biblical in approach. And secondly, we are dealing with problems raised by the occult and must therefore be on our guard against being side-tracked or bogged down.

Presentation

The section dealing with the occult has been placed in the middle of the evening, and should be treated as far as possible in a matter-of-fact, informative way. Avoid time-wasting discussions about the occult: 'Have nothing to do with the fruitless deeds of darkness, but rather expose them. For it is shameful even to mention what the disobedient do in secret' (Ephesians 5:11–12). Our task is to expose the occult for what it is, give the course members sufficient confidence to deal with common presenting symptoms of the occult, and move on quickly as we 'find out what pleases the Lord' (Ephesians 5:10).

Use should be made of an OHP or flip chart summaries. See Appendix G. Remember that there is a lot of ground to cover, so try to keep a balance in terms of time spent on each part of the session.

Start the section dealing with helping those involved in the occult with praise, followed by prayer for both guidance and protection. Possible hymns are: 'Jesus the name high over all'; 'Lord, the light of your love is shining'; 'At the name of Jesus'. You could finish the section with a hymn of adoration, eg 'Holy, Holy, Holy is the Lord'.

▶ Guidelines for good practice

Background information

This course is mainly designed to help congregations build up effective teams of people who can minister to individuals who seek help with the various 'dis-eases' of their lives. Sometimes this ministry will take place within the context of a specific healing service (see next session), but more often than not it will take place informally during, or more probably after, an act of worship of the congregation.

The Churches' Council for Health and Healing has produced some guidelines for good practice for those involved in the Christian healing ministry. The report *A Time to Heal* sets out the House of Bishops' draft guidelines for those in the healing ministry. What follows here relies heavily upon these documents. We need such guidelines to protect those who come to us for help, to safeguard those who minister and to protect the reputation of God's church.

Good guidelines not only have to be practised, but they have to be seen to be followed. Remember the last words of Paul's discussion about spiritual gifts in 1 Corinthians: 'But everything should be done in a fitting and orderly way' (1 Corinthians 14:40). When people see that we have general guidelines and codes of conduct they will be more likely to entrust themselves to our ministry.

The following five points (OHP 12, Guidelines for good practice) will cover some of the issues raised:

1. The priority of mature Christian spirituality
2. The importance of working in teams
3. The demands of confidentiality
4. The necessity of supervision
5. The need to be aware of your limitations

1. The priority of mature Christian spirituality
The example of Jesus is set out clearly in Mark's 'sample day' in the Lord's life in Mark 1:21–39. After a day spent in teaching and healing, Jesus retired to bed, only to get up 'very early in the morning' to find a solitary place to pray. We are to be channels of God's healing love and power and this love and power can only flow from us insofar as we allow it to flow into us (John 7:37–38). Regular, methodical Scripture reading, regular times of prayer, times of 'seeking the Lord', regular participation in the sacrament of Holy Communion, regular reviews of our life, and the confession

of our sins, are all part of this spirituality. Note the emphasis on regularity; our whole life should be one which seeks to live in God's will.

This is not a list of irksome duties, but a liberating way of living which transforms us, so that we can bring God's transformation to others.

2. The importance of working in teams
There is a biblical precedent for working in teams in Luke 10:1, where Jesus sends out the 72 in pairs. Working together:

- protects us from spiritual pride;
- gives us mutual support;
- demonstrates that we are acting as the body of Christ;
- defends us from compromise which might arise if we were alone with an individual.

In practice, teams of two or, at the most, three people, where both sexes are represented, have been found to be a good safeguard.

3. The demands of confidentiality
Maintaining confidentiality becomes more difficult when using teams, but all those involved in ministry should keep strict confidentiality. Do not gossip or let details of any conversation slip out carelessly, particularly in prayer meetings!

4. The necessity of supervision
It should be widely known that all those involved in the church's ministry are supervised. Normally, in the context we are discussing, the supervisor will be the minister of the church. We note in Luke 10 that after 72 had been sent out, they returned to 'debrief' with the Lord (Luke 10:17).

It is important to avoid the 'confidentiality trap'. Be very careful how you respond to a person who says, 'Promise me that what I tell you will be in the strictest confidence.' They may be about to 'dump' on you something that you cannot handle. The proper response to such a request should be along the lines of, 'Obviously we minister under strict guidelines of confidence, but we do have supervision, and very occasionally we might need to refer something we have been told to our supervisor. This is rare and I will inform you immediately if we enter an area of exploration which might require this course of action.'

5. The need to be aware of your limitations

In the account of the healing of the boy with an evil spirit there is a salutary phrase: 'I begged your disciples to drive it out but they could not' (Luke 9:37–45). We need to recognise that we can't handle everything. Knowing when to hand on a client to someone with greater expertise in a particular area is an essential part of good practice.

Prompt referral may be vital. It is not a cop-out to ask someone, 'Have you seen your doctor about this?' If necessary, do all in your power to help them pluck up courage to follow this up. Some team members may wish to consider further training after this basic course (see next session) in areas like listening skills, care of the bereaved, and so on.

Praying with children

Wherever possible, parents or guardians should be involved in praying with children. You may also be able to encourage the parents themselves to pray for the children on a more regular basis. However, we must also recognise that children are individuals and may wish to seek ministry alone. Wherever possible this should be done with the parents' knowledge and consent.

Every church should have in place a policy about the children in its care. This policy applies as much to the healing ministry as to the youth club. The Home Office's *Safe From Harm* will give further help in this area. The following points should be borne in mind:

- Respect the child's trust in you. Don't give promises you may not be able to keep – especially in the area of confidentiality (see above).

- If a child discloses details of abuse, do not ask questions. Offer a simple prayer of peace and protection for the child, and refer the matter to the minister. Advice should be sought from your local Social Services department. Never launch into private investigations.
- Often children come asking for prayers for other members of their family. Explain that our prayers will bring Jesus close to those for whom we are praying. Avoid quenching the natural faith of the children, but at the same time be careful not to build up false expectations.

Laying on of hands

It is not necessary in every prayer situation to lay hands upon the recipient. An informal, gentle touch on the shoulder may be more appropriate than a more formal laying on of hands on the person's head. Bearing down on the top of a person's head is very oppressive; it is better to lay one hand gently on the top of the forehead, and the other at the back of the head. This is a supportive and less oppressive position.

Touching of an area which is the focus of the prayer may be done if modesty permits. Sometimes it is appropriate to ask the person being prayed for to hold the affected part while hands are laid on the head.

The following points should always be borne in mind:

- The person's consent should be obtained and it should be made quite clear what you intend to do.
- It is helpful to mention that there may be outward signs of the Holy Spirit's power, like a sensation of heat or tingling. The absence of such signs does not mean that the Holy Spirit is not active in the situation.
- Only lay on hands with prayer if a third person is present.
- Avoid any action that might be misconstrued.

▶ Areas which can cause concern

Introduction

Most people who become involved in the Christian healing ministry eventually find themselves facing a situation where those who come for prayer for healing may need some form of deliverance ministry. We base our belief that malign forces exist on biblical evidence and human experience.

> 'As we read through the Gospels we cannot help but be struck by the extraordinary numbers of references to Jesus confronting Satan and the whole realm of demons. A major theme in the New Testament is the clash between the kingdom of God and the kingdom of Satan. The climax of human history, in fact, occurs when God, in Jesus, overpowers Satan and frees the human race from Satan's domination.'
> (Francis MacNutt, *Deliverance from Evil Spirits*, Hodder and Stoughton 1996)

Those who have become involved in occult practices potentially expose themselves to demonic forces. It is not possible to know how badly a person is affected by any occult activity. Many become involved at a very minimal and casual level, while others get sucked in to a much deeper level.

We can help those who have been involved in complementary medicine or malign healing practices in the following ways: (refer back to Session 3, 'Alternative therapies'):

- Listen carefully *without condemnation* to the individual's account of what alternative or complementary therapy they have been using.
- Ask how they feel about their therapy now. They may feel OK about it, or they may be having doubts about its efficacy and have turned to Christian healing. They may realise that they have been led by subtle pressure into activities that are condemned in Scripture.

- Gently challenge practices that are condemned in Scripture, such as the involvement of mediums or spiritism.
- Pray secretly that the Holy Spirit will lead the person into all truth.
- If they come under the Holy Spirit's conviction, lead them to repentance, confession and God's forgiveness.
- Bind any lying spirit that might have been involved. Seek appropriate help to deal with any deliverance that might be deemed necessary. (In an Anglican church the minister should be informed, and he or she will follow the guidelines laid down in the diocese.)
- Be calm and at peace. Trust in the Lord. Do not overreact.

Group discussion

→ Jane has recently joined your church. She claims that she was healed during a seance. The medium 'called up' a famous nineteenth-century doctor who brought about her healing. She would like to tell her story at the next healing service. 'My painful knee got better instantly. My story would give people faith to be healed,' she argues.

How would the group dissuade her from this action? Bearing in mind that this experience was very precious to her, how would you help her understand the Christian perspective on her healing? How could this be done without her feeling a sense of rejection?

Helping those who have been involved in the occult

People quite often seek ministry after they have:

- used ouija boards;
- used tarot cards;
- consulted a palm-reader or astrologist;
- become obsessed by occult games (eg Dungeons and Dragons);
- had contact with spiritists, or been involved in seances;
- experienced some frightening or strange phenomena, such as poltergeist activity;
- been involved in cults of one kind or another;
- taken part in witchcraft practices;

- become victims of curses;
- been involved in Satanism.

Quite clearly the level of involvement differs greatly, and those who wish to help must be aware of the guidelines, particularly the value of working in teams, the importance of supervision, and the need to be aware of our limitations. Sometimes mental illness can mimic demonic influence.

Introduce OHP 13 which shows two underlying principles when dealing with people who claim to have been involved in the occult.

1. Just because we cannot see something, we must not assume that it does not exist.
2. Just because we can see something, we must not assume that we understand it fully.

Jesus saw the effect on the boy with the evil spirit in Mark 9, and addressed the spirit, which was unseen but none the less real. Part of the Western modernist worldview which influences our thinking denies the reality of anything which cannot be tested, measured or seen. We are moving out of this era of thinking today, into a postmodern culture. Here it is all too easy to fall into the second extreme of believing anything.

Take, for example, a person who has had experience of some sort of poltergeist activity, like electric lights switching on mysteriously, or movement of inanimate objects. Because they have 'seen' things happening and there is no rational reason, it is all too easy to assume that it is the work of ghosts or spirits. In fact there is a large body of evidence to suggest that such activity is linked to repressed emotional and psychic disturbance in people.

In dealing with these matters we must be careful to avoid an unbelieving sceptical rationalism, or at the other extreme, an unthinking and gullible acceptance of a 'supernatural' reason for a phenomenon.

Group discussion

→ Tom has suffered from depression since his wife, Mary, died two years ago. He was introduced to a woman called Myrtle who said she could contact his wife. Tom saw Myrtle as a caring and kind person. However, he thought that contacting Mary was wrong, believing that his wife should be 'left in peace'. Myrtle heard about Tom's depression and contacted him again saying that Mary would not be at peace until Tom had recovered from his depression. Myrtle wants to arrange a 'meeting' so that Tom can be reassured that Mary is all right and consequently healed of his depression. Myrtle claims that this will make Mary happy, too. Although not a churchgoer, Tom remembers that after Mary's funeral the vicar had said, 'If you need help at any time please get in contact with me.'

Discuss what might be happening in the spiritual realms here. How can Tom best be helped?

Summary

The danger is to overreact when people come to us saying that they have been involved in the occult. However, as soon as we know what we are dealing with, we should silently:

- bind any dark forces so that they can harm no one;
- ask the Holy Spirit to lead us into all truth;
- pray for the protection of Jesus, and the angelic forces.

We should then:

- listen without condemnation;
- discover how the client feels about their involvement, and whether they want to repent of it;
- avoid fruitless and exhausting arguments about rights and wrongs;
- remember the ten principles listed below;
- seek further help.

Optional material

The following principles are listed in Appendix E of the link-work books. It may be enough at this moment simply to draw attention to them.

Ten principles when helping people who come for prayer after they have been involved in the occult:

1. Enthrone God, not the 'principalities and powers' (Deuteronomy 20:1–4; 2 Chronicles 20:15).
2. We minister from the victory of Christ; we do not fight for a victory (Colossians 2:13–15; John 12:31).
3. Rely upon God's active help through his word (Luke 4:1–13); his authority (Luke 9:1–2); his gifts (1 Corinthians 12).
4. Do not let the devil set the agenda. The team makes the decisions about the timing and ministry style. Buy time by binding any spirits so that they can cause no harm until appropriate ministry is available. At the same time, signal to the person coming for prayer that they are being taken seriously.
5. Work in teams – this avoids spiritual pride and false accusation (Ephesians 6).
6. Do not overreact. Most people coming to faith today have been involved in the occult at some time. Not all unexplainable phenomena are of the devil! Avoid at all cost terms like 'possession' and 'exorcism'. Be aware that mental illness can produce very bizarre behaviour.
7. Deliverance is into Jesus as well as away from evil.
8. Realise that there are degrees of occult influence. Much is fairly minor, but occasionally we can encounter more serious manifestations where the victim is no longer free to be the person God wants them to be.
9. Know yourself and recognise your limitations.
10. Operate within the framework and guidelines of your church. In the Anglican church such matters must be referred to the parish priest, who will seek guidance from the bishop or his representative in this ministry.

The following table illustrates various levels of dark influence and the suggested appropriate ministry. It is a gradual progression, and hard and fast distinctions are impossible.

General category	Type of behaviour	Appropriate ministry
Area 1	Temptation (this is not the same as sin)	Prayer
	Sin	Simple, personal confession to God
Area 2	'Besetting sin' (a continual problem)	Confession and counselling
	Compulsion	Counselling and healing of the memories
Area 3	Oppression	Professional counselling and breaking of any curse
	Infestation	Professional and expert counselling and deliverance
	Personality take-over	As above, with psychiatric advice

Area 1 should be within the scope of a small team praying with people after a service. Area 2 will involve people who have had specific training in counselling, with the local church leader acting as supervisor. Area 3 will involve advice from outside specialists. (Within the Anglican church each diocese should have at least one ordained priest who can act as an adviser.)

The local team will be active in making the right contacts, binding with prayer any suspected evil influence, and supporting the person who comes for prayer, spiritually and emotionally.

▶ When the Holy Spirit comes

Those wishing to explore the methods of prayer for healing developed by John Wimber would do well to go on one of the special courses arranged on this whole subject. Group members should be informed about the sort of outward, visible signs that may accompany a 'power encounter' with the Holy Spirit. If they are to develop this style of prayer for healing, further teaching will be necessary and is readily available both through courses and on video.

John Wimber taught that there are five steps in the healing process:

1. The interview.
2. The diagnostic decision.
3. Deciding which type of prayer to use.
4. The time of prayer, which will often include outward manifestations of the work of the Holy Spirit.
5. Directions on how to follow up the time of prayer – what people should do to keep their healing and what they should do if they are not healed.

Signs that may accompany prayer are:

- Eyelids fluttering; shaking (particularly hands); tingling or a feeling of 'electricity'.
- Sense of heat or sometimes cold. The latter is not necessarily a sign of evil.
- Deep breathing or panting.
- Sobbing or laughing. This is often a sign of deep emotional healing taking place and may well break out spontaneously on occasions over a period of some days or even weeks after the prayer session.
- Hot spots – often an indication of where hands should be laid. (Some ministers find that if they 'scan' the back of a person who is asking for prayer, they sense heat in one place which is nearly always at the epicentre of the person's pain.)
- Glowing – a glistening on the face, often accompanying a sense of heat.
- Dizziness, light-headedness, being 'drunk in the Spirit'. People will sway and, if standing, will sometimes fall down.
- Screaming and crying out. This is often mistakenly thought to be demonic activity, but is more likely to be a release of repressed emotions of hurt, pain or rage.

- Deep peace and joy, and an 'encounter' with the Lord in the depths of a person's being.
- If there has been occult activity, the person may well go rigid and the body contort.
- When demons are present there may be guttural language, often obscene, and often accompanied by mocking taunts like 'You will never get rid of me.'
- Sometimes the person may appear to 'rest' – this can be a ploy to stop the ministry continuing.

One of the main insights which the Lord seemed to bring to those who were influenced by the so-called 'Toronto' experience was the value of praying several times for a deep release of the Holy Spirit. It seems that if a person is prayed with each night for a week, they are able to allow the Holy Spirit to minister in a more profound way than if there was just one time of prayer. The 'Toronto' experience allowed people to receive the blessing of the Holy Spirit with more frequency and intensity.

Optional teaching

People have 'preferences' in their spirituality. Some are alarmed by outward, visible manifestations, and some find a contemplative approach threatening. OHP 14 points out in a very general way how Luke, Paul and John had different preferences about the work of the Holy Spirit. We need all three strands in our church life, but they may not be contained in any one person. This insight has helped congregations come to understand that people can hold different preferences about the way the Holy Spirit works, and helps to avoid the sad divisions that can occur in this area.

See OHP 14: Different emphases of New Testament writers on the work of the Holy Spirit.

- Luke concentrates on outward, visible signs of the Holy Spirit's activity.
- John concentrates on the inward, spiritual reality of the Holy Spirit's activity.

● Paul is concerned to show how the Spirit works for the good of the church, in the life of the church.

As we proceed with this ministry we must pray continually for the guidance of the Holy Spirit and reassure any who might be disturbed by outward manifestations.

Group Bible study – the prayers of Jesus
➔ Examine the prayers and words of command of Jesus in the following accounts:
  ● Matthew 8:3; 8:16.
  ● Mark 1:25; 10:52.
  ● Luke 13:12; 17:14.
  ● John 4:50; 5:8.
Note the variety, the brevity and the authority.

▶ Ways of praying for healing (8)

The prayer of command

As we learn to accept the power and authority which Jesus gives his disciples, we may find ourselves being led into prayers of command. Here we are not asking Jesus to heal, but standing in the sure knowledge that we act with his authority, and in his power we command a sickness to leave, or a person to be healed.

The Bible study showed us the brevity and authority of many of the prayers that Jesus spoke. Of course, the whole of the life of Jesus was prayer, and we must not infer that these simple, direct sentences represent the whole of the prayer that Jesus offered in his heart and mind to his Father. However, the words are the outward, visible signs, and certainly the prayer of command features in them.

Under the guidance of the Holy Spirit command prayers may be used in the following ways:

● To a person – 'Stretch out your hand.'
● To part of a person's body – 'Back, I command you to be healed.'

- In the 'binding' of satanic powers.
- In the breaking of curses.

▶ Worship and prayer

After dealing with the material presented in this session, it is helpful to end with worship in which Jesus is lifted high in our praise. He has already won the victory, and our praise honours this fact. You could use such songs as 'Lift up your heads', 'To God be the glory' and 'For I'm building a people of power'.

Preparation for next session

If you are planning on Holy Communion or the Breaking of Bread at the end of the next session, warn group members that the time will be extended. An extra half an hour has been built into the provisional timing for the next session.

Resources for Session 8

- OHP diagrams for this session:
  - OHP 12, Guidelines for good practice
  - OHP 13, Helping those who have been involved in the occult
  - OHP 14, Different emphases of New Testament writers on the work of the Holy Spirit
- Ministry in practice source material:
  - *Guidelines for Good Practice for those involved in the Christian Healing Ministry.* This includes a Code of Conduct and is published for the Methodist Church and the Churches' Council for Health and Healing by Methodist Publishing House, 20 Ivatt Way, Peterborough PE3 7PG.
  - *A Time to Heal*, Appendix 1, pages 293–327. (Note particularly pages 325–327.) The House of Bishops' draft guidelines for good practice in the healing ministry. The small handbook *A Time to Heal* prints these as pages 51 and 52.
  - John Wimber, *Power Healing*, Hodder 1986.
  - John Richards, *But Deliver us from Evil*, Darton, Longman and Todd 1974.

- Michael Perry (ed), *Deliverance*, SPCK 1996. This is based on practical experience of the many church advisers in this ministry and reminds us of the rational approach often needed.
- John Woolmer, *Healing and Deliverance*, Monarch Books 1999.
- When faced with children who disclose disturbing material contact your local Social Services department, or get in touch with the NSPCC on 0800 800 500. This is a 24-hour national helpline in the British Isles. Alternatively, Childline, on 0800 1111, is a 24-hour free confidential counselling service.

9 Moving on in the Christian ministry of healing

 Aims

- To introduce course members to some specific ways of praying for healing, in particular the healing of emotions and memories.
- To examine ways in which the local church may move forward in this ministry.

 Outline and timing

You will need to decide in advance which parts of the main learning focus are appropriate for your group. The whole session may be slightly longer than normal, depending upon how you decide to run the final act of worship and fellowship.

0–15 mins	Getting started
	● Short review
	● Opening worship
15–60	Main learning focus: Moving on in the healing ministry
	● An introduction to the healing of emotions and memories.
	● Going further. Possible avenues for people to follow.
	● Establishing a healing ministry in your local church (optional)
	● The healing of the congregation and the church as a place of wholeness.
	● Should we have healing services? If so what form should they take?

60–120   Final act of worship (possibly to include Holy
              Communion)

 # Running Session 9

God is calling his whole church, not just individuals, to this ministry. If this is a new idea to your church then quite a large part of the evening could be spent on the question of where God is leading the church at this moment. Is God calling you to set up healing services? If so, what sort of services? You might feel it important to convene a special meeting or meetings to think through your parish policy with regard to the ministry of healing.

However, it is quite possible that you are using this course in a church which already has an established healing ministry. In this case, time may be profitably spent on looking at how each member of your group feels they fit into the pattern established in the church. Do they have any particular skills? Are there areas of ministry in which they would wish to gain further training (eg, listening skills)?

Intercession lists

It will be very important to go carefully through the list of people for whom you have been praying over the past eight sessions. There will be cause for thanksgiving for perceived answers to prayer, and maybe the need to work through some cases where there does not seem to have been an answer.

Final worship

The final time of worship (which could be followed by an informal party) might take the form of a service of Holy Communion. You will have to allow time for this in planning the evening. An extra half an hour has been allocated for this final session.

Preparation

- Pray for all those you expect to come.
- Have large sheets of paper and coloured markers for group work and for other notes or lists.

- Prepare OHP acetates.
- Any special arrangements for the final session?

▶ The healing of emotions and memories

What is sometimes known as inner healing is 'a process of emotional reconstruction experienced under the guidance of the Holy Spirit'.
(Ruth Carter Stapleton, *The Experience of Inner Healing*, Ecclesia Books 1977)

The process involves:

- discovery;
- owning the past;
- prayer reconstruction and ministry (where appropriate);
- debriefing and after-care.

This topic can raise anxiety in some people. Questions asked often reveal this. For example, people will ask: 'Should we dabble in psychology?' 'Isn't it manipulative?' 'Is it scriptural? I don't see Jesus doing it.' 'Isn't it a form of hypnosis?' 'I've heard of people feeling worse after such prayer. How can it be good?'

See OHP 15: The action of the Holy Spirit in the healing of memories.

The illustration represents a whole personality. The part above the horizontal line represents what is known (the conscious mind) and the part below the line what is hidden (the subconscious).

The Holy Spirit will 'lead us into all truth' and one way he does this is by gently lowering the threshold of the known/hidden divide. (This is represented in the diagram by the large dark arrows pressing the dividing line down.) Ideally this is a natural and gradual process, but the misuse of drugs, hypnosis and some occult practices can lower this threshold by force.

The dark blotches represent the unpleasant parts of our character, and the evil things that have happened to us. Some are remembered but many are hidden. As our defences are lowered – represented by the dividing line – so more of this material is revealed. Some of this will be 'of the light' and some 'of the dark'.

This explains why it is that when the Holy Spirit is invited into a person's life they are often convicted of sin. Some of the dark bits that have long been locked away begin to surface. As this happens, the Holy Spirit begins the process of sanctification by gently pouring his healing love and power into these now exposed areas. This is represented in the diagram by the smaller white arrows and white areas where past hurts have been healed.

Because God allows us to keep our free will, he will never force us to lower the defence line – it must be with our willing co-operation. We who minister in this way must keep a respect for the freedom and integrity of the individual, and not be manipulative.

Person-centred prayer ministry

John Leach of Anglican Renewal Ministries has developed a way of praying for the healing of memories which avoids being manipulative. At every stage the person seeking ministry is empowered – not the minister. He suggests the following sequence:

1. Ask the person seeking ministry to identify the issue.
2. Then she/he is invited to think of an image of God which speaks to the situation. What is the significance of this particular image?
3. The person seeking help is asked to identify the place where God is acting and the significance.
4. The Holy Spirit is 'invited' (ie, his presence is acknowledged) to take control of the ministry.
5. The person seeking ministry is invited to offer a prayer in their own words about the issues revealed.
6. The minister prays.
7. A time of silence to wait on the Holy Spirit to minister.

8. Feedback – the minister asks if anything significant has happened.
9. The prayer time ends with a blessing or maybe returns to step 2 for further discovery.

John warns ministers against talking too much, imposing their own ideas and agenda, sharing words or pictures too quickly or adding to the seeker's images. The whole focus is on letting the Holy Spirit and the seeker take the initiative.

This model is clearly explained in detail in a pamphlet published by ARM called *Person-Centred Prayer Ministry*, by John Leach.

Group activity
→ Share in pairs a vivid childhood memory. The memory does not have to be an unpleasant one but do not tell the group this fact at the moment. After a few minutes return to the plenary group to write a list of the headings of the memories (eg, my birthday party when I was five; being lost at the zoo; falling off my bike and breaking my arm).

Now ask the following questions:

● Did any group members assume you meant bad childhood memories?
● Why do you think people often assume that bad memories are asked for?
● Are bad memories more vivid than good ones?

Ask the group to make a list of the most common childhood events that can lead to emotional damage. The following summary may be helpful but try to draw this from the group. Some common types of events that lead to emotional sickness and may be healed by the Spirit through the 'healing of memories' are:

● being lost, feeling abandoned or rejected;
● feelings of worthlessness implanted by ambitious parents and teachers;
● childhood sexual abuse leading to sexual, emotional, physical and spiritual problems;

- various childhood traumas, eg hospital and dental procedures in childhood;
- unfulfilled teenage idealism and ambitions;
- bereavement and losses experienced during the formative years and later.

It is important to stress that healing of memories is not hypnosis, nor is it a destroying of memories. It is rather a bringing of suppressed (deliberately forgotten) and repressed (a reflex action to forget) events into the light of Christ for his healing (John 16:13; 8:31–38). Truth is 'facts in perspective'. The healing of memories helps us to see the facts of our life from the perspective of the healing power of the Holy Spirit.

Caution: It would be wise to say that any prayer for the healing of emotions and memories should be done by experienced and trained people. However, part of the healing process is to let people talk about past memories, provided there is no coercion. Do the listening; get help with the ministry if you do not feel confident!

The role of forgiveness in the healing of memories

Forgiveness often plays a very important part in the healing of memories. First, the client may need to confess wrong attitudes within themselves, and possibly wrong actions remembered from the past. This may be done to a priest within the sacrament of confession, but can also be done within a more informal setting of ministry.

Second, the person must be prepared to forgive those who have hurt them. However, it must be stressed that some trauma is so destructive that the person will not be able to forgive. In this situation they may be asked to pray for openness to God's grace to forgive.

'God has poured out his love into our hearts by the Holy Spirit, whom he has given us.'

(Romans 5:5)

Part of God's love is his forgiveness, and so we can rely on God's power to forgive if we feel unable to do so ourselves. The important thing is the desire on the part of the person to forgive. There may well be a need at this point to display physical and emotional signs of this catharsis. We should not be alarmed if the person sobs, shakes or even screams. Such activity in this case is not demonic but the natural outpouring of hurt that has long been repressed.

Setting people free

Healing of memories is also about cutting people free from roots that are bearing destructive fruits. For example, some people have over-demanding parents. Such people may become over-anxious to please. They feel that God is totally unreasonable in his demands on their life. The only way this wrong thinking can be helped is for them to be 'cut free' from the original cause.

Some people may need to be cut free from the effects of occult involvement (see Session 8). Group members should be reminded always to refer such cases to their minister or church leader. Remind people that we fight from the victory that Christ has already won over the powers of darkness on the cross.

▶ Going further

This course is designed to be a starter kit. Its aim is to help ordinary members of churches to minister competently to others, but of course it also opens up the possibility of further study and specialisation.

However, doing courses can be addictive! Jesus used an apprenticeship model when he trained his disciples. The apostles and early Christians did not spend their lives going on courses! Hopefully your group members have come on this course so that they can get on and pray for others to be made whole by Christ, and are expecting to see 'the Lord working with them'. I would suggest that it is important to really try to put into practice right now in your church what they have learnt on this course.

There is a bewildering array of courses which could follow this one. Group members may need advice to help them decide which, if any, they should follow up. Encourage them earnestly to seek God about this: 'Find out what pleases the Lord' (Ephesians 5:10). They may discover as they start to pray regularly with the sick that they have a special call, for instance, to the healing of memories. This may be an indication that the Holy Spirit is calling them to follow up this line of further study.

If group members feel led to specialise in some way, it should be discussed with the church leadership, who have an overview of the needs of the congregation.

Optional section – establishing a healing ministry in your local church

Much will depend upon the situation in the parish or church where this course is being held. Should there be no formal healing ministry at the moment, then time spent on trying to discern the will of God using the following step-by-step procedure will be valuable.

Group discussion
→ Do we feel God is leading us towards a healing service?
- Who are we aiming at in such a service? A small interested group within the congregation, the congregation in general, or people outside or on the fringes of the fellowship? A congregation-focused healing service may well use Communion services as a basis, but if the aim is to attract a more diverse congregation then thought should be given to some simple form of Service of the Word (*Patterns of Worship*, page 325, 'A service of healing'). See also *Common Worship Pastoral Services* Part One, 'Wholeness and Healing'.
- What should be the frequency of such services? Here again much will depend on your individual situation. A healing service held once a month on a week night has the advantage of being a regular feature, but can degenerate into a holy huddle which you cannot stop once started. On the other hand, a well publicised service about once a quarter works quite well

if there is opportunity for further ministry at other times of worship within the church. Such services act as a reminder to the church that Christ is present to heal whenever his body meet for worship.

- Who will minister at such services and what style of ministry will it be?
- How will such people be chosen and authorised?
- What safeguards and systems of review are to be put into action?

The church as a place of wholeness

Healing, particularly relational healing, must be an ongoing concern of any congregation where the healing grace of Christ is outpoured.

> 'Follow the way of love and eagerly desire spiritual gifts.'
> (1 Corinthians 14:1)

Henri J. M. Nouwen in his book *In the House of the Lord* (Darton, Longman and Todd 1986) speaks of fear being the great enemy of intimacy. Fear, he says, 'makes us run away from each other, or cling to each other but it does not create true intimacy'. If the church is to be a place of healing it must provide a warm, accepting and intimate atmosphere, but one in which everyone can still retain their individuality. Cloying ministry, feeding the hidden needs of the minister, destroys the healing atmosphere as surely as self-centred indifference.

OHP 16: The church as a place of healing

- The architect – God's plan for the church.
- The foundation – we build on the foundation of Jesus Christ.
- The power supply – the power of the Holy Spirit.
- The bricks – the people of God.
- The mortar – love, forgiveness, goodness, gentleness. care and ministry.
- The welcoming place – first impressions.

- The cleansing place – forgiveness, healing of past hurts, deliverance.
- Room for living – healing should free people to be what God intends them to be.
- The feeding place – what is our spiritual diet?
- The resting place – the balance between activity and passivity. Exhausted Christians are a bad witness to the healing ministry!
- The sending place – encounter with the world, healing and evangelism. Addressing the causes of dis-ease in our world.

Group activity
➔ Use the OHP as a discussion starter about your own local church as 'a place of healing'.

A sample church policy (optional)

A sample church policy is given in Appendix E. This might provide some help if you are setting up a formal healing ministry within your church.

▶ Worship at the final session

There is much to be said for a special celebration for the last session. (See *Saints Alive! Life in the Spirit* for a more detailed treatment of how to run the final session.) Allow extra time for this celebration. This would enable you to have an informal Communion service and some teaching about the healing power of the sacraments, or teaching suited to your own church tradition.

▶ Conclusion

This whole course should be seen as a 'starter kit' in the Christian ministry of healing. If it has provided a stimulating foundation to your group's thinking and experience of this wonderful ministry, it will have been worthwhile. Give thanks to the Lord. It is my prayer that through this course many more Christians will be encouraged to 'preach the kingdom and heal the sick'.

Resources for Session 9

- OHP diagrams for this session:
  - OHP 15, The action of the Holy Spirit in the healing of memories
  - OHP 16, The church as a place of healing
- Moving on source material:
  - Ruth Carter Stapleton, *The Experience of Inner Healing*, Hodder and Stoughton 1978.
  - Mary Pytches, *Yesterday's Child*, Hodder and Stoughton 1990.
  - Russ Parker, *Forgiveness is Healing*, Darton, Longman and Todd 1993.
  - Russ Parker, *Healing Dreams*, Triangle 1993.
  - John Leach, *Person-Centred Prayer Ministry*, Anglican Renewal Ministries 2001.

A The accounts of healing in the ministry of Jesus

Special events	Matthew	Mark	Luke	John
Man with unclean spirit		1:21–28	4:31–37	
Peter's mother-in-law	8:14–15	1:30–31	4:38–39	
Man with skin disease	8:2–4	1:40–42	5:12–14	
The paralysed man	9:2–8	2:3–12	5:17–26	
Man with withered hand	12:9–14	3:1–6	6:6–11	
Gadarene demoniac	8:28–34	5:1–17	8:26–39	
Woman with chronic bleeding	9:20–22	5:24–34	8:43–48	
Syro-Phoenician woman	15:21–28	7:24–30		
Deaf and dumb man		7:31–37		
Blind man		8:22–26		
Child with evil spirit	17:14–18	9:14–27	9:38–43	
Bartimaeus (sight restored)		10:46–52		
Centurion's servant	8:5–13		7:1–10	
Dumb demoniac	9:32–34			
Blind and dumb demoniac	12:22		11:14	
Woman bound by Satan			13:10–13	
Man with dropsy			14:1–4	
Ten lepers			17:11–19	
Malchus's ear			22:49–51	
Nobleman's son				4:46–53
The cripple at the pool				5:1–15
Man born blind				9:1–7 ff

Summaries of healings				
After the Sabbath	8:16–17	1:32–34	4:40–41	
Many demons		1:39		

	Matthew	**Mark**	**Luke**	**John**
Multitudes follow Jesus	15:30	3:8–10	6:17–19	6:2
A few miracles	13:58	6:5–6		
'All who touched him'	14:36	6:56		
A summary before teaching	4:23		6:17–19	
'Go tell John' many healed	11:4–5		7:21–22	
Crowds	9:35		9:11	
	14:14		5:15	
	19:2			

Raising of the dead

Jairus's daughter	9:18 ff	5:22 ff	8:40 ff	
Widow's son			7:11–17	
Lazarus				11:1–44

B An imaginative prayer journey

After a time of praise, bring the group to stillness. This can be helped by asking the members to sit as still as they can, to focus on their breathing, to be aware of the sounds in the room like the ticking of the clock. After a suitable time ask the Holy Spirit to touch the imaginations of those present:

> Come, Holy Spirit, and touch our imaginations with your loving power. Protect us from any evil influence and fill our minds with new insights of the love of our heavenly Father, through Jesus Christ our Lord.

Then ask the group to imagine that they are wandering round a general hospital. As they walk along the corridors and wards they see suffering in many forms. For example, a youth in pain just after a motorbike accident; a bewildered old man hearing the news of his wife's death; a frightened child; a harassed doctor; a cleaner who has just been told that she is to be made redundant. (Don't describe the people in too much detail; let the Holy Spirit inform the imaginations of the group.) Widen the idea of suffering to include areas of pain which are not medical.

Focus the attention of the group on the signs that direct people round the hospital. For example, to X-ray, to the Intensive Care Unit, to Maternity. Then ask them to imagine a sign labelled 'To the pain bearer'.

They follow the signs and finally come to the door marked 'The pain bearer'. They knock on the door and are called in. They enter.

Ask them to imagine what lies beyond the door. Keep silence for several minutes.

Read Isaiah 53.

After a while ask the group to 'come back' into the present, and allow time for people to speak about what they imagined or felt. It is most important after such a prayer journey to allow people to speak about their experience if they so wish. Be very accepting and affirming of all the comments. Some people may find such an exercise a 'silly game', while others may be deeply moved by the experience. There are no right or wrong answers. Ask people not only what they imagined, but how they felt in that situation.

C An alternative Gospel meditation

It is most helpful in getting to know Jesus to use imaginative meditations, putting oneself in the place of one of the people Jesus healed. There are several different ways of doing this, but here is one of the simplest.

Rewrite a Scripture passage by changing the pronouns which refer to the person being healed into the first person. Not every passage is suitable, so you will have to look at them in advance. If you are using group members to lead this meditation you will have to see that they are well prepared before the session. It will probably mean that you will have to write the passage out. Thus Luke 5:12–14 would read:

> While Jesus was in one of the towns I came along, covered with leprosy. When I saw Jesus, I fell with my face to the ground and begged him, 'Lord, if you are willing, you can make me clean.' Jesus reached out his hand and touched me. 'I am willing,' he said. 'Be clean!' And immediately the leprosy left me. Then Jesus ordered me, 'Don't tell anyone, but go, show yourself to the priest and offer the sacrifices that Moses commanded for your cleansing, as a testimony to them.'

The passage needs to be read well, with plenty of time for the words to have an impact on the listeners. After the reading keep silence for several minutes, then allow people to offer vocal prayers.

It is most important after this to allow the group to discuss how they felt during this meditation, and what difference the simple changing of the pronoun made to them. Encourage those who found it helpful to use the same method themselves in their own prayer times.

D Praying for people to be filled with the Holy Spirit

If you have a copy of the Leaders Manual for the *Saints Alive! Life in the Spirit* course, read through the notes for Session 6. Obviously each leader must pray for members of the group as he or she feels led. The following order has proved useful in some situations, particularly for Anglican group members who are used to fairly formal worship in their local church.

Prayer of commitment

Leader:	Do you turn to Christ?
Response:	**I turn to Christ.**
Leader:	Do you repent of your sins?
Response:	**I repent of my sins.**
Leader:	Do you renounce evil?
Response:	**I renounce evil.**

Heavenly Father, I want to belong to you from now on. I want to be freed from the dominion of darkness and the rule of Satan, and I want to enter into your kingdom and be part of your people. I will turn from all wrongdoing. I ask you to forgive all the sins that I have committed. I offer my life to you, and I promise to obey you as my Lord. I ask you to baptise me in the Holy Spirit and to release the gifts of the Spirit in my life. In the name of Jesus. Amen.

After the prayer has been made allow time for all the group members, under the direction of the leader, to pray for the person. Be relaxed, be full of praise, be expectant!

Group members may wish to discuss this prayer privately with the leader of the group, and some may feel led to make a full sacramental confession of sins some time before making the prayer. In particular, involvement in other non-medical methods of healing which are contrary to Scripture, particularly those based on the occult, must be renounced totally. Our healing is in the mighty name of Jesus Christ and in him alone.

E A sample church policy

We believe that prayer for healing is part of the ongoing Christian ministry of the church. We ask the church leadership and congregation to accept the following policy document. This is Christ's ministry and we are called to be channels of his healing love and power by our prayers and actions.

1. The Christian ministry of healing is part of the whole life of the church, and involves both expectant prayer in the power of the Holy Spirit, and loving pastoral care.

2. This ministry is to be seen as part of a total ministry towards wholeness, which includes the ministry of other caring professions, particularly the medical profession.

3. The ministry will have a particular focus at acts of worship where there will be the proclamation of the gospel and prayer for healing with laying on of hands for those who wish to receive this ministry. These services will take place (frequency) at (date and time).

4. It is proposed that these services be simple so that those who are unfamiliar with church services will feel welcome and at ease.

5. Ministry will be led by those in church leadership, using teams of church members. These members will be chosen for each occasion by those leading the service and it is expected that such members will have attended training sessions.

6. In addition to occasional services with prayer for healing, teams of church members will be available after every main public act

of worship to minister to those who need specific prayer. They are not counsellors, but have a role of prayer befrienders. They will be answerable to the church leadership, who will act as supervisors.

7. We are all involved in helping to create within our church a welcoming and healing atmosphere and it is our individual responsibility to act with love, care and forgiveness to one another.

8. The work of the healing teams and the frequency of the special services will be reviewed annually, and modified where appropriate.

9. All taking part in this ministry are asked to study the guidelines of good practice and to ensure that such guidelines are always followed.

F Commissioning a ministry team in a church

This prayer has been used at the end of the main service in an Anglican church every Sunday to commission a group of two or three people, drawn from a pool of about fifteen, as ministry team for the day.

It has had the effect of making it quite clear to the congregation that this is part of the ongoing work of the church. It involves the congregation because they are part of the commissioning, which is open and public. The limited authorisation is for that particular day only, and in no way implies that the team are gifted 'healers'. It is expected that all team members will have been through some basic training like *Saints Alive! Healing in the Church*.

Using a fairly large number of people on the rota for the ministry teams has avoided people being used too often, and also shown that this is a ministry which is potentially for every Christian.

One of the team is appointed to take responsibility for the ministry. They are prayed for before the last hymn of the service, standing at the front of the church so that everyone in the congregation can see who is on the team for that day, and feel part of the commissioning.

The prayer

Our Lord Jesus Christ sent out his followers with his power and authority to heal the sick and to proclaim that the kingdom of God had come. In his name, and on behalf of this congregation, we authorise you to minister to those who come to you today.

May God the Father, Son, and Holy Spirit, fill you with his love and power. Amen.

G Overhead projector acetate masters

The healing process analysed

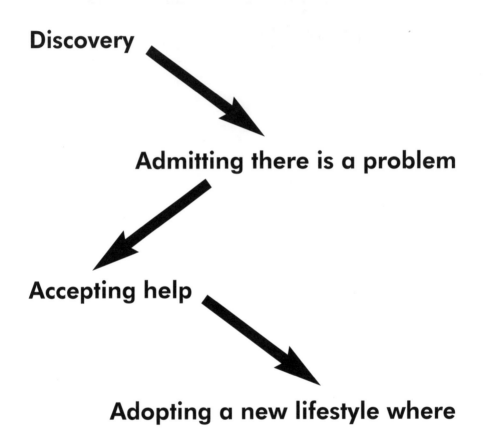

Discovery

Admitting there is a problem

Accepting help

Adopting a new lifestyle where necessary

The wholeness diagram

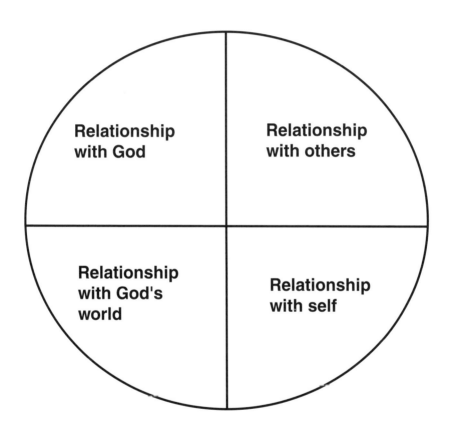

Fragmentation
overlay

The laying on of hands with prayer

WITH

Prayer

Care

Other people present

Gentleness

Awareness

God's love and God's power

WITHOUT

Being oppressive

Being dominating

Being abusive

Views about healing

'Booster rocket'

A SPECIAL POWER GIVEN BY GOD TO GET THE EARLY CHURCH STARTED

'Saints and shrines'

GOD DOES HEAL BUT AT SPECIAL PLACES THROUGH SPECIAL PEOPLE

'Sacramental'

GOD'S HEALING COMES THROUGH THE SACRAMENTS OF THE CHURCH

'Every-member ministry'

ALL ARE CALLED AS DISCIPLES TO THIS MINISTRY

'Faith healing and psychic gifts'

POPULAR VIEW HELD BY MANY AND ENCOURAGED BY THE MEDIA

Alternative medicine – a Christian approach

- Is the method in line with biblical teaching?

- Does the 'patient' come into any form of 'bondage' to the therapist?

- Are the gullible exploited?

- Are unconscious minds exposed to unknown powers and forces?

- Is there any contact with spirits or any form of spiritism?

- Does the 'healer' claim to have special healing powers?

- Are unknown spiritual forces used?

- Does the technique employ pseudo-scientific jargon or procedures?

- Does the method produce a greater overall freedom and harmony for the client?

- Do you have a sense of unease in any way about the method?

Faith when things get tough

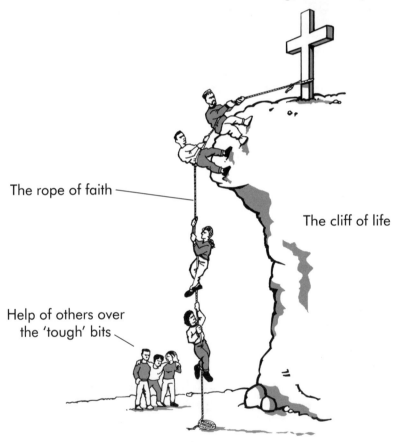

THE CROSS
(Our only security is
to know God's
saving love for us)

The rope of faith

The cliff of life

Help of others over
the 'tough' bits

Our pilgrimage together

OHP 6

Balance in the healing ministry of Jesus

Balance

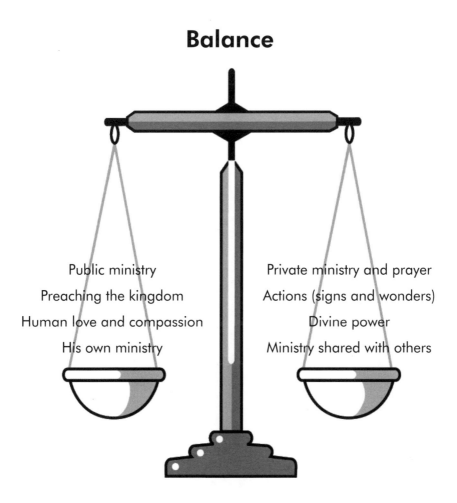

Public ministry	Private ministry and prayer
Preaching the kingdom	Actions (signs and wonders)
Human love and compassion	Divine power
His own ministry	Ministry shared with others

Balance between evangelical and pastoral approaches to healing

The church needs both!

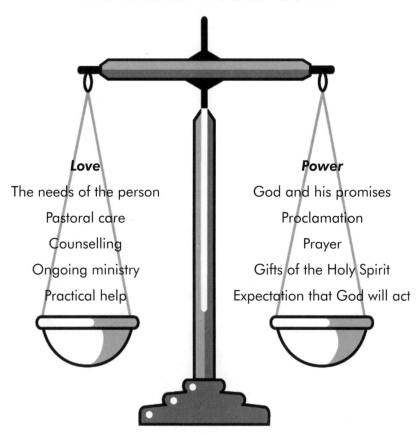

Love

The needs of the person

Pastoral care

Counselling

Ongoing ministry

Practical help

Power

God and his promises

Proclamation

Prayer

Gifts of the Holy Spirit

Expectation that God will act

Filled with the Holy Spirit

Five key biblical instructions

Thirst   John 7:37

Repent   Acts 2:38

Ask   Luke 11:9ff

Believe   Mark 11:24

Obey   Acts 5:32

The mystery of suffering

If God is all-powerful and all-loving why is there suffering?

Human sin and evil accounts for some suffering but not all

Why are some people wonderfully healed, but others are not?

What is our attitude to death?

'The God we serve is able to save us . . . But even if he does not, we want you to know, O king, that we will not serve your gods' (Daniel 3:17–18).

Why some are not healed

1 Lack of faith

2 A false value placed on suffering

3 Sick person called to redemptive suffering

4 Sin in patient or minister blocking prayer

5 Not praying specifically

6 Not praying to the real cause of the sickness

7 Refusal to see God's healing in medicine

8 Not taking care of our body

9 Now is not the time

10 A different person called to pray

11 Environment prevents healing

Guidelines for good practice

1 **The priority of mature Christian spirituality.**

2 **The importance of working in teams.**

3 **The demands of confidentiality.**

4 **The necessity of supervision.**

5 **The need to be aware of your limitations.**

Helping those who have been involved in the occult

'The occult' – that which is hidden

Two important guidelines

1 Just because we cannot see something, we must not assume that it does not exist.

2 Just because we can see something, we must not assume that we understand it fully.

Different emphases of New Testament writers on the work of the Holy Spirit

St Luke

is interested in outward visible signs of the Holy Spirit's activity.

St John

concentrates on the inward spiritual reality of the Holy Spirit's activity.

St Paul

is concerned to show how all this works out for the good of the church, in the life of the church.

The action of the Holy Spirit in the healing of memories

The horizontal line represents the conscious/sub-conscious divide.

The Holy Spirit gradually depresses this line as our 'defences' come down.

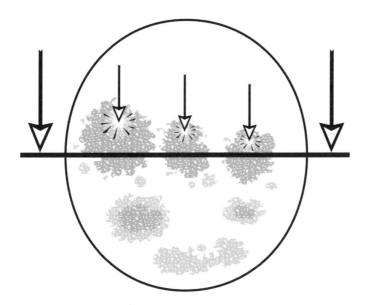

This reveals hidden memories and hurts which through prayer ministry (smaller red arrows) the Holy Spirit touches and transforms with God's healing love.

The church as a place of healing

THE ARCHITECT – God's plan for the church.

THE FOUNDATION – Jesus Christ.

THE POWER – the Holy Spirit.

THE BRICKS – the people of God.

THE MORTAR – love, forgiveness, goodness, gentleness, care and ministry.

THE WELCOMING PLACE – first impressions, the porch, welcomers.

THE CLEANSING PLACE – forgiveness, healing of past hurts, deliverance.

ROOM FOR LIVING – healing should free people to be what God intends them to be.

THE FEEDING PLACE – what is our spiritual diet?

THE RESTING PLACE – exhausted Christians do not witness to the healing ministry!

THE SENDING PLACE – encounter with the world, healing and evangelism. Addressing the causes of dis-ease in our world.

SAINTS *alive!*
Life in the Spirit

This course has already been used by more than a quarter of a million people. Now fully updated, it is an ideal way to help bring renewal into the life of the church. It has proved useful for people who are –

- enquiring about the Christian faith
- seeking deeper commitment
- exploring the work of the Holy Spirit
- preparing for baptism or confirmation

Saints Alive! Life in the Spirit offers a nine- or ten-week teaching programme on topics ranging from 'What is a Christian?' to 'What are the gifts of the Spirit?'. It has been used around the globe by churches from a variety of denominations.

A link-work book is available for each course member, as well as a video.

John Finney and **Felicity Lawson** wrote the course when working together in a church in Nottingham. Since then John has served as the Church of England's Officer for Evangelism and then as Bishop of Pontefract before retiring in 1998. Felicity was Dean of Ministry and Director of Ordinands in the Diocese of Wakefield and is now Vicar of Gildersome in Yorkshire.